BUSHVILLE

For all my girls—
Nina,
Jeannie & Meg, Savannah,
Beth, Stacy & Kate & Corinne,
Susan, Eileen & Elena, Tess,
Ally & Ashton,
Anna in Barcelona —
and all their beloved boys.

For the players,
in memory of Joseph James Murphy (1883–1934).

BUSHVILLE

Life and Time
in Amateur Baseball

by
Jerry Kelly

McFarland & Company, Inc., Publishers
Jefferson, North Carolina, and London

You can discover more about a person
in an hour of play
than in a year of conversation.
Plato

♦

Let's play two.
Ernie

Library of Congress Cataloguing-in-Publication Data

Kelly, Jerry, 1953–
  Bushville : life and time in amateur baseball / by
Jerry Kelly.
    p.   cm.
  Includes bibliographical references and index.
  ISBN 0-7864-0979-7 (softcover : 50# alkaline paper)
  1. Baseball.   I. Title.
  GV867.K45   2001
  796.357 — dc21   2001031264

British Library cataloguing data are available

Manufactured in the United States of America

Cover photograph by Jerry Kelly

*McFarland & Company, Inc., Publishers
  Box 611, Jefferson, North Carolina 28640
  www.mcfarlandpub.com*

CONTENTS

1

OPENER

Opener

You may have done this once yourself. You pick up an old baseball and roll it around in your fingers as if you've never felt one before. This ball has been bashed and battered, left out in the rain, clawed by a raccoon and sniffed by a stray cat. What was once pure white horsehide is now parched and weathered, blackened by earthly elements and partly peeled back. Some of the 108 red stitches have loosened and frayed, and one of the ball's sides is now a flap, inviting you further in. So you sit down and work on it, holding it between your feet and using both hands to peel it apart. With earnest work you can get it done, removing two elongated figure-eights of hide and unwinding yards of wool and poly-cotton thread until you get to the core, the "pill." Red rubber, black rubber and cushioned cork comprise this inner ball. If you were somehow to get that open, you'd find the center of a purposeful career, now over. In its glory days this ball was chased by players eager to hold it and pass it between themselves, making a game of its flight. For as long as it held together it has occasioned stories and glories, locating specific fame and oblivion. Never touched by a big league player, it carried the game's narrative nonetheless in soul campaigns known as local ballgames.

Chuck Moore chucking, the author at short (courtesy of Anthony Frascello) 1992.

State

It's a hand-eye game that you play with your feet. Basically that, and more. A contest always and never quite the same, whose best players play best by doing things the same way every time, but in the long run with variations and sure imperfection.

At its fluid essence an ebb and flow of power, position and finesse creates baseball's enduring moment — where players find themselves in the game's grip, gripping it and releasing it, holding it and throwing it, hitting it and catching it. A baseball is a token passing through eternity from its moment of game blur to its spot on your shelf. You should own one, as just such a token. Maybe you do.

The game of baseball is a fine construct. Its trace through anyone's life can range from a youthful diversion to a full-blown career, a tender small-fingered grasp to a deep muscular understanding. It provides a focus and a way to express the physical self in a physical world. I've played every moment of my games as an amateur in my favorite sense of that word — doing something I love, just for the love of it. The roots of that soulful effort run as deep as my earliest memories, measuring them. And possibly, yours likewise.

There are things to note and stories to tell — always and never quite the same, like all of the other threads of the game. Bushville is as much a state of your mind as mine. Its places and plays connect us.

◆

I've been trying to recall the first time I saw it — that expanse of the empty lot beyond our backyard. It typified the burgeoning suburbs of early 1950's Long Island, near the south shore. Now a waving sea of tall grasses, in our youngest days it was a bare, broad trough carved out by bulldozers to create a drainage basin and to provide earth for an adjacent hillside leading to a highway overpass. The slender valley thus created was just broad enough for a small ballfield, a squeezed diamond with narrowed proportions. If you imagine it to be Yankee Stadium (as we did, then), my bedroom window was the Bronx House of Detention — close enough to gaze upon the field in darkness, a short sprint away as morning dawned and we were set free.

From the time I was six years old, this state property adjacent to the highway hillside (we called it "State") both contained and opened the game of sandlot baseball for our neighborhood full of kids. Its free air released us from the watchful eyes of parents and the twin prisons of home and school. We carved out a classic oblique diamond within it, wearing baselines in the dusty grasses of this sandy salt marsh bedded with clay. The field configuration was off by a lot — we chose to squeeze the field into the slender valley so we'd have deep (if narrow) outfields, keeping the steep right field hill (and the stream running along its base) out of bounds. In time we'd remake the field into a truer diamond, incorporating the stream and the hillside into a short-porch stadium right field.

The chain-link fence separating our yards from State was a tough, scraping climb for a six-year-old, but in time it became an easy vault. As the number of eager neighborhood ballplayers swelled, our sand-lot games evolved from self-hitting to lob pitching to full-bore, fast-pitch battles. Not one adult was ever involved. We could gather two full teams of kids almost any time, and make do with less. In our imaginations we were the Yankees—perennial late-fifties, early-sixties champions swaggering through endless delicious innings of crisp and graceful play.

Our baseball world was boosted into high gear by the arrival of two new kids in the neighborhood, fresh from New York City and asphalt baseball glory. Robbie Fitzsimmons was a year older than me — perhaps eight when I first saw him — and his brother Ronnie was three years older still. They moved into a ramshackle house nearby with their younger sister and mother. Alice Fitzsimmons was a tough, resilient woman whose husband had left her with these three kids. In the early 1960s, "broken" families were uncommon in our parts. Robbie told everyone his father was in the navy, out to sea, and we believed him for as long as he needed us to.

On the ballfield, the brothers Fitzsimmons were a spectacular pair — playing the game with passionate authority. They quickly took charge of the rag-tag troops and formed us into a winning team. We went to work on the field, raking and picking rocks and planting grass seed. We hijacked lawn mowers and used them to chop down the tall weeds in left field — leveling small shrubs by hoisting a roaring mower up and heaving it on top of them. Our fingertips were spared by the grace of their smallness, and game strength. We dug our dugouts by hand with shovels and rakes, right there in the clay. But most importantly, we reoriented the field to make it a true diamond, with right field running straight up the hill to the highway guardrail, and a deep left field that cried out for a homerun wall.

By propping up old mattresses and box springs that had been dumped over State, we erected the requisite outfield fence in left. We

scrawled the Yankee Stadium dimensions on it with magic markers—
301 down left, 457 in the left-center "Death Valley" alley, and 463 in
dead center. In right field we had the hill to contend with, so we lined
up two-by-fours halfway up, making any ball hit beyond them a homer.
The hill presented a natural stadium effect, affording a sense of enclosure and a true Yankee short porch in right. The highway atop the hill
represented River Avenue and the elevated Lexington Avenue Express
of the South Bronx. We could picture hundreds of fans filling the
bleacher hillside of our spectral stadium, even when it was really just
three little sisters screeching.

Robbie Fitz — a small lefty like Whitey Ford — pitched, while Ronnie played shortstop or second base with the flair of an all-star. Being
older and bigger than most of us, Ronnie inspired awe with mighty
strokes of his bat. He could switch-hit, and the right-field hill was an
easy lefty shot for him. He idolized Bobby Richardson but swung for
the fences like Mantle, and was our regular three-hole hitter and
absolute leader.

Robbie competed with his older brother for our allegiance, but also
served as his lieutenant by organizing raids on the local five-and-ten
for sporting goods. We'd file through the cramped store and exit as a
group, contraband ballcaps on our heads and shiny baseballs stuffed
in our shirts. Robbie once limped out with a bat crammed down each
pants leg, tipping yet another new hat to the clerk on the way out.
Another time he juggled three new balls out the door while the rest of
us jostled to buy bubblegum — at a penny a pop, about the only thing
we ever paid for. None of these missions were undertaken merely for
the thrill of stealing. We had real needs— balls wore out, bats broke,
and, lacking uniforms, we had to at least wear uniform hats. At one
point we used the magic markers to scrawl pinstripes on our T-shirts,
but the next wash cycle took them away. Anyway, all of that was window dressing. What mattered most was going back on popups, turning two, and putting the ball in play with runners in scoring position.
Under Ronnie's guidance we did all of that very well.

A case in point: late in a close game against the Pat Drive Rangers—
another rag-tag neighborhood team from the other side of the hill —
we have runners on first and second and nobody out. I get a lob pitch
on the outside half of the plate and dribble a slow roller to second.

With the runners in motion there's no chance for a double play, so they take the easy out at first. One down, second and third. Robbie follows with a drag bunt back to the pitcher, who holds the runners, but his distracted throw fails to get Robbie at first, so the bases are loaded. Ronnie steps up to the plate lefty, flexes his arms, and drives a low meatball up to the top of the hill for a grand slammer. His home-run trot is like Mantle's—a quick limping sprint, shoulders proudly squared, head down, soaking up the cheers from the assembled throng of little sisters. We mob him at home plate and dowse him with a shaken bottle of 7-Up.

The crowd in our head roars.

Gladiators

They were Huck and Tom with beguiling smiles. When the Fitzies arrived on the Gladstone Avenue scene, they drew us in like moths to night-game lights.

Their T-shirts and rolled-up bluejeans, dirty Keds, well-broken mitts and lively eyes bespoke an appetite for mischief. They were loose cannons compared to the rest of us—sometimes Alice was gone for days and they'd eat cookies and drink Coke for breakfast, watch as much scratchy TV as they wished, and tempt us with misadventure. Our parents often forbade us to play with them — usually after an incident like when Robbie pegged another kid in the head with his BB rifle (his defense: "I only pumped it twice!"). But then, after things died down a bit, the Fitzies would come over to our yard and charm their way back in, and we'd get tacit permission to resume their companionship (with provisos and prohibitions). It was moot — we played with them anyway. But they did their charm-school number to meet us halfway, giving in to our parental limitations, and in the end we'd play "run-the-bases" after supper in someone's front yard, screaming for the ball with darkness bearing down and a runner sliding in.

♦

On hand for the Fitzsimmons invasion was a ready cast of characters. There were some good budding ballplayers whose fathers and Little League coaches were drilling them in the game. My father was never much for the game, but the Gladstone Gladiators (as we knew ourselves) made up for that.

I can picture the whole crowd now over State on a humid summer day — Ronnie holding court while Robbie tried desperately to wrest our attention. Willie Walsh playing hard, intense and angry, with Danny Collins— a lefty first-baseman — showing his smooth glide in whatever he did. These were young boys, but practiced into a real readiness. We were bolstered by a few 15-year-olds, Ronnie's pals— most notably Bird Sherwood,* another poor and rugged kid with big holes in his sneakers and a mighty swing. At six feet and 220 pounds, Bird was a Babe Ruthian presence; he once gobbled 13 hotdogs from the blind old vendor up on Union Street in rapid succession, gulping down each one with a loud burp and "Hey friend, do it again," mimicking radio commercials of the time for "Ballantine — Ballantine Beer!" He could hit the long ball, too.

Others played starting (if not starring) roles— me behind Ronnie (sometimes literally) at second base — Richie Seitz light-footed at the base of the right field hill, and Robbie scampering across center when he wasn't pitching. Richie Siegel was a bit younger, but limber and willing wherever we put him. For a brief while there was Jimmy Gray,* an accomplished thief who could do little else very well. Jimmy wanted onto the team badly, telling Ronnie he'd steal anything we needed in exchange for some playing time in left field. Ronnie ordered up a backstop, a real home plate, a pitching rubber and some bases. And to our amazement Jimmy delivered, recruiting some hooligan pals to help drag all of the above from Morton's Day Camp down by the bay. We had to hide all of it in the woods so the state cops wouldn't see it when they parked up on the hilltop to watch us play. Jimmy Gray got some innings, but was a far better thief than an outfielder.

Dominic Sivillo caught, and sometimes played third. Willie played third and sometimes short. Ronnie played short and slid over to second for lefties. Danny caught everything at first. We could all hit lob pitching, and we scored runs in bunches.

---

*Throughout this book, I've used real names with the kind permission of those named. Where it seemed more fitting, I used nicknames instead of real names. This is, after all, a baseball book, and what's baseball without nicknames? (You know who you are.)

In the instances where I've had to use a fictional name, its first occurrence appears with an asterisk.

Our games against the Pat Drive team took on the spectral quality of a championship season. Time after time we beat them, seldom
losing a game. We handled another team from up Bird's way, and a
third from the other side of the tracks. We were on the "good" side,
but barely; commuter trains and slow-rolling freights shook our houses
day and night, embedding their vibrations in our baseball bones.

The Union Street Boys posed another challenge. They were not a
baseball team, but a gang. They were older — most of them Ronnie's
age or more — and were what we called "hoods" — they greased their
hair, drank beer, smoked, and fingered their girlfriends by moonlight
on our outfield mattresses. We rarely saw them by day. But late one
afternoon we've got the whole team there, doing batting practice, when
they part the weeds and step out, the whole surly gang of them. The
Union Street Boys wasted no time taking charge, grabbing our bats,
waving us out to the field, declaring they were playing us and batting
first.

We huddled at the mound. Ronnie looked us all in the eye, steel-
ing us to go ahead and show these hoods some hardball.

The Union Street Boys batted like a bunch of lollygaggers, lurch-
ing at lob pitches out of the strike zone and hitting slow rollers, jogging toward first in their Cuban heels with cigarettes dangling from
their mouths. We took offense at their surly-yet-giddy disregard for
the game and our stadium. Another look from Ronnie swept across the
infield, and through the dugout when we trotted in for our at-bats.

We massacred them in the bottom of the first. They didn't get an
out. We pounded the ball and took the extra base. We stole home,
cheering bitterly, pissing them off royally. They started knocking down
the mattresses, and Ronnie threw his mitt down in the dirt to declare,
Enough. We squared off to fight, and Willie drew the first punch from
one of the larger hoods. He immediately sprinted off homeward, which
they taunted, seeing it as retreat; in fact he was going for reinforce-
ments. Ronnie squared off with two hoods, taking and giving punches,
not backing down. The rest of us shifted around them warily, spitting
and shouting, taking some hits and giving some. I wouldn't call it
a brawl, exactly — better ones came later — but more of a meandering
fistfight punctuated by lots of shouting. Kind of a standoff, curiously,
given they were so much bigger and supposedly tougher. But then with

a battle yell here comes Willie with a crew of older guys in tow — clean-cut football players who lived up his end of the block. The Union Street Boys take off at a dead run and our whole crew, now nicely reinforced, chases them for almost a mile across the tracks, up to Sunrise Highway, catching a few and delivering some football-style retribution.

After that episode, our troubles with the Union Street Boys (and their sister gang, the Union Street Girls) continued, but within new limits. It became routine — we'd reset the mattresses every morning and start the game. But they never showed up to play us again. We had settled that issue; over State, we owned the daylight.

♦

We spent an eternity on that field. Its ruts never improved much, but we learned how to play it, and suffered remarkably few injuries upon it. Visiting teams were generally not spared — this was a tricky surface in the extreme. You had to be part mountain goat to play right field — what with the stream and then the steep hillside — and nowhere was the field smooth or green or grassy. One year we planted grass in straight rows, one seed at a time, thinking we'd achieve the Yankee Stadium look; but the sand and clay would have none of it, and today it's hard to find any evidence of the game there. Saplings now crowd the right field hillside, and new kids have worn dirt-bike paths across the infield and out to left. It's an empty little sump, overgrown with tall brown grasses— a thundering echo as trains rumble by and the wind bends the tall weeds.

Grounders

I've heard it said, "I'll eat anything doesn't eat me first." Baseball ate me first. Like a sort of food chain, the game has always fed me while consuming me. All down the line, it's provided things to chew on — ways to have ideas with muscles, to communicate with eyes and fingers, and to process life's disorder in an ordered, exciting, unpredictably nourishing manner.

Take these two groundballs, from memory: the first is off my bat over State, at the ripe old age of eight. It's rolling toward a kid named

Henry — the tall and lanky ten-year-old shortstop for a team from across the tracks. He wears the semblance of a uniform, as do all his ragged teammates. In slow motion, the groundball bounds across the sandy clay of our makeshift field, with Henry bent and waiting. In slower motion, I'm sprinting off toward first but watching that grounder all the way. Henry's watching it too, and he's ready, but fate takes a turn as it can and does in this game — the grounder finds a rock then, with a bad hop, it locates Henry's so-called nuts, bullseye. No one wears a cup on this field; it simply isn't done. Henry's lights are out before he even hits the ground. His teammates carry him home like a big sweaty rag-doll, his arms limp.

Another bite: it's two years later, and my first Little League try-out on a real field. For years I'd negotiated State's bad hops with its broken glass and detritus, but this was different: a real mound, green grass, white bases, straight white lines, and a grown-up coach screaming at me to "stay low, stay down!" The grounder approaches in the same slow motion that so captivated Henry, and finds its own rock. This bad hop is higher, missing my nuts but finding my newly-minted front teeth. Smack, to dust. I'm spitting out blood and bits of enamel while spinning around looking for the ball. The coach, now bellowing like a mule, gallops toward me at shortstop with an astonished look and a gaping hee-haw mouth. I find the ball that ate me, pick it up, and as I taste blood I realize what a great whistler I've just become.

Two casualties. Brothers in battle. Both taken by a fate that consumes young men and keeps them young, sometimes far beyond age. Baseball can claim you, and not let go easily. There are reasons for that. By way of memory: two grounders rolling across time, in slow motion, with the bright sun lighting them up and taking us down.

♦

I'm in my late forties now, and nearing the point of giving up the ghost. A shoulder injury has dogged me the past two winters, despite relentless rehabbing. The mind is willing but not like it once was, and the body's clearly reluctant. This may be the spring to finally downshift to softball, relegating this baseball season (and all futures) to the sidelines.

But that's not for sure, yet. There's reason for one more go, if I can find the sharpness to do it. The risks are more injury and the prospect of going out sloppy — leaving the game with sour memories, glory going over to repeated abject failure. Spoiled meat. I've already swallowed some of that.

So it hangs in the balance, now. If I can rehab the arm and bring the body back, I'll be out there again next summer on Sunday afternoons and Thursday nights, feeling the flow of electricity the game generates from the inside. That's where I most want to be, and what I most fear losing: that sense of place in the circuit, with the power that flows through players. It's an artful balance of science and soul, sinewy music with fine rhythms and a clear lyric. It's an ever-changing matrix, a big green semiconductor of infinite action pathways, curves arcing in the third dimension across the diamond's surface and players' souls.

Simply this: for those of us who found it and kept at it, the game characterizes what and who and where we are, our lifetime, like nothing else we have. Simply that.

Get-Go

I came to the game young, and have stuck with it more or less forever. Aside from a few years lost to injury in my early twenties, I've always played. And now there's this accumulation of issues — some clearly personal, but all shared by many other players and fans. In those issues I find the time to contemplate the glorious run of the game as well as the end of my run, just up ahead. Working your way down the ladder at the end of your playing days — from any level — presents such an opportunity. Cause for reflection.

The issues that characterize baseball are manifest in other realms of human drama, straight across the board. Love and purpose, and devotion. Focus. All that comprises the flow with which human life progresses when it's involved — thoroughly engaged — in any meaningful activity, whether making art, designing algorithms, gardening, parenting, or just being a functional person in a day-to-day world. All of that is apparent in the game, if you look at it closely and see it broadly. Inside the game, the flow is ever-present and always elusive.

It comes down essentially to consciousness, and the patterns we build with it upon the world. Baseball's patterns reduce some of that to abstraction, statistic, and melodrama. But they also construct life as an ordered occasion of real effort, physical and mental and emotional, and the possibility of real active legend. Over and over, heroics and defeat, gain and loss. It's figurative of other essential activities that issue from our collective life and consciousness.

When viewing anything through a specific lens, there's the trap of fashioning a focus that clouds the periphery. Some of us who love the game are tempted to elevate it to a mystical method, twinkling with near-religious meaning. It can get like that. In fact it's hard to avoid, because there is so much played out in the game's course. It's a well-developed system in human terms, with flow potential actualized every day of every season.

But it's important to locate the game in its real occasion, as thousands of amateur players do on thousands of simple diamonds all over the place. Next time you fly anywhere over the U.S., look down and count the ballfields. Driving through suburbs and small towns during baseball season can bring you upon a game, and a companion sense of delight in finding its rituals happening in a particular place and time with all possible attention to its protocols and a local accent.

Playing as an amateur for forty years brings me this attachment to baseball's best moments— instants when game recognition and game sense come together and fall apart with a racing heart and keen, definitive performance — at all levels of play. That's what defines the game, from the inside.

Our habit of picturing ourselves through the lens of television isolates Major League Baseball as something apart, tiny and self-contained in most fans' lives— an edge vehicle. It's a virtual reality more than an actual one (existing in effect or essence more than in actual fact or form). As happens with most of what TV touches, the screen subtracts too much of the whole view. On that flat narrow plane, nothing much really happens—certainly not the panoramic spectacle of real baseball. The view from the couch voids the scope and variety of the game, reducing it very seductively by subtracting too much.

But it's possible to locate baseball elsewhere, in the endless color of invented amateur space. The local game delivers on its promise as it's played, personally and with great democracy, across this nation and around the world. There are many stories to tell. And now, as Casey might have said, you could look them up.

Peripatetic Career

Year	Team	Position	League
1953	Home	Fetal	Rookie
1958–67	Gladstone Gladiators	2b	Neighborhood Sandlot
1963–65	Lions Club Lions	2b, SS	West Islip Little League
1966–68	West Islip Lions	OF	Junior High School
1969–70	West Islip Lions	OF	High School Varsity
1971–79	Interregnum: nine vagabond seasons away from the game		
1980–83	Gladstone Gorillas	2b	Fast-Pitch Softball
1984–85	Smithtown Bulls	2b, SS	Fast-Pitch Softball
1984–85	Shoreham Mets	2b, 3b	LI Stan Musial League
1985–89	Stony Brook Cardinals	2b, OF, P	LI MSBL Charter Team
1986–89	Smithtown Cardinals	2b, SS, 3b	LI Stan Musial Snowflake League
1990–91	Brentwood Yanquis	2b, SS	LI MSBL
1991–94	Oyster Bay Bombers	2b, SS, 3b	LI MABL
1994–96	Kenyon College Lords	2b, 3b, P	NCAA Division III
1996–98	Columbus Angels, Warthogs, Angels	2b, SS, P, C, 1b, OF	Columbus MSBL Columbus MSBL
2000	Columbus Wolves	2b, P	Central Ohio MABL

My playing days span neighborhood sandlot, junior-high and high-school varsity, then nine seasons spent away from the game after a hobbling injury in my high-school senior year. I picked the game up again in my late twenties, playing modified fast-pitch softball with the Gorillas, then graduating back to baseball with George and the Cardinals, then with the Shoreham Mets, the Brentwood Yanquis, the Oyster Bay Bombers, the Kenyon College Lords, the Columbus Angels and Warthogs, and finally now the Wolves.

How many teams, how many games, innings, pitches? Too many to count, but never enough to feel final. The blessed continuity of pulling on the gear, walking out into the sunlight and doing the constant dance that never quite repeats has the weight of the new all around it, and deep echoes in the present tense.

Middle infield was where I was born and always lived. Playing second base gave me my game — that off-angle on righties and dead pull from looping lefties. The center of the diamond is where basepaths angle off and energy turns. A winning game swirls around second base; a loser never gets there, or dies there.

As a second baseman you own that pivotal bag — it's yours, and no runner is entitled to it. So you focus on keeping it (or making it) vacant. It's a great feeling to pick a runner off at second, and, when it happens, it's usually the work of the catcher, not the pitcher. We picked a guy not long ago in a Warthogs game against the Gray Sox — I saw him taking a big lead at second and not hustling back between pitches (his team down by 9 runs, go figure). So I stood there at my normal second base position, facing our catcher Scott Anders with my arms hanging, and just wiggled my right index finger. Quick, just one time. After the next pitch Scott stands up slowly as if to throw back to the pitcher, but instead rears back and throws a seed to me at second. We have the guy picked by five feet. It's one of those drive-the-stake-in-the-heart sort of plays, putting a punctuation mark on our domination of this game. Down the road, in a closer game, that play might save us.

Turning two is a lifelong practice (never perfected) courtesy of two heroes: Bobby Richardson of the early '60s Yanks personified by Ron Fitzsimmons of the Gladstone Gladiators, same years. The double play is not just a pitcher's best friend, it focuses the infielders on their own capability, and builds the kind of rhythmic confidence through the middle infield that makes a winner. You play infield with your feet — the hands are easy. Baboon (of the Gorillas) used to say I'd catch anything if I left my feet, meaning if I dove for it I'd get it. I brought down two line drives my first game back with them, and the second one got us out of a jamboree.

You have here a righty singles and doubles hitter, with a decent stroke to right on the outside pitch and occasional power to pull on the inner half (but also beat there a lot). The right-field gap is my double, my plateful of ribs. Slower hands now, weakened ankles, and suddenly a sore right shoulder. It's looking mostly rear-view, from here.

♦

In my kitchen I have an old sepiatone photograph of my grandfather, Joe Murphy, standing in an empty lot on the upper west side of

Manhattan circa 1910 in his baseball uniform. He seems comfortable, his weight shifted to his right leg, his right arm hanging low. It's the game that brings him home to his skin and senses—you can see confidence of place in his face.

Times do change. But that comfort hasn't changed a whit. It is the keeper — grace shifting from leg to leg, balanced for eternity.

2

THE BRINK

Aperture

Hopping the fence of a summer morning, we skip through a tangle of wet weeds and sprint out into the opening field, feeling the day bursting with possible treasure. It was like that — moments surging toward the first throw of the day, and through to the last. One by one each player arrives with a yelp, and before long, infield practice has broken out while three outfielders arm-wrestle over a broken bat and a roll of shiny black electrical tape. Life is one long happy argument — let's turn TWO, NO let's do infield-in throws to the plate, NO let's start a game now. Who bats first? ME — NO me — no ME — OK, you THEN me. Somehow we manage to settle things peacefully as the field opens wider and wider, minute by minute.

The Brink

It's a game of thresholds. As player or fan, we're brought again and again in the course of innings to the brink, where situations are set up and resolved in motion — by clutch hits and brilliant plays in the field, by gutty pitches and good swings, or by a fielder losing his sense of where he is and where the game is turning, or a baserunner finding himself suddenly in no-man's-land. The game does turn as we cross those occasions, leaping to our feet with cheers, or our shoulders sagging as we watch a teammate disintegrate and a three-run lead dissolve.

West Islip Lions strategizing 1963.

There are larger thresholds to cross with the game. We grow with it as a changing constant, watching it unfold, brooding over it, quickening our steps across a parking lot on the way to the ballfield or stadium. From early youth to beyond the great beyond, it continues.

Being a fan of the big league game is engaging, but ultimately passive for most. On the other hand, if you play the game as you age, you traverse boundaries that measure you, lending focus to the use of your athletic soul with counterparts — kindred spirits and competitive others. The efforts involved in being an older amateur player are considerable, the returns momentous. Your sense of the game grows even as your physical skills diminish. You accommodate loss with measured gain and clarifying pain, playing the game with more of your self in order to stay competitive. Some guys get better in their thirties than they ever were. It can happen.

Within the game, the thresholds are clear as they've always been, measured by distances from base to base — from third to home, from second to home, from first to third — those key position and power shifts that comprise a game. The lead-off at first, and at second, and third (with a run on the brink). Such sudden turning moments of win and loss carry us over definitive boundaries, as in our Bombers game with the Dominicans at Bay Park one howling late-summer night in 1994. With the game on the line, their leftfielder pulled down Joe Arena's liner to the fence, our winning run dying at second base. Joe blistered this particular low fastball — a rocket-shot liner still rising when the fleet leftfielder pulled it down, his ass to the plate and his glove arm as long as it had ever been. I can see the play now as clear as night, and feel the thudding implosion as our runners pulled up to a stop and defeat dawned on us.

Starter

This is a baseball life — and even as it winds down, it accelerates in understanding and involvement (coaching kids, playing sloppy softball, and staying in shape to give hardball one more season or one more injury, whichever comes first). I've played more baseball than I can clearly remember. As much as anything else in this amateur life, it's what I've been doing.

It's a baseball life for others, just as surely. Some are professionals who get paid to play the game. They're paid a little in the minor leagues, much more in the bigs (six figures for rookies, seven for vets, eight for stars — that's millions of dollars per season, guaranteed, whether or not they play a single game).

For big league players, it's a rock-star kind of life on its surface (on TV) even as it's all hard work every day of each long season. It's a constant battle to bring their best forward and keep the physical spirit working. The game demands that. Even as you make it up the ladder, dominating at each level of competition, you still have to produce to keep your place. And it can be gone in an instant, all guarantees notwithstanding.

You play as long and hard as you can, and eventually yield your spot to someone else. It ends. And thus, the farther the road goes, the more vivid and vital the games become. That's just as true for those who play the game for the sheer love of it — the amateurs (from the Latin word amator, for lover). I've been one of those ever since I picked up a baseball and felt its stitches and smooth curves. The hooking flight of a baseball across a diamond creates a swirl of action that pursues us and pictures us in its progress. It delivers you across a definitive arc of your own self, if you attend to it. Like most things in life it's a mixed blessing, from start to finish — glorious in its power to lift us up and put us back down.

In Spirit

So here's to all the fans and amateur athletes who love the game, actively. That's love as a verb, an action; actually, a series of actions spanning a length of time — a season, or a life.

Here's to the spiritual side of the game. There is one. Its edges exist just as surely as the chalk boundaries. The game breathes with its players, with its fans, and with all who engage it at any level. Those who play experience the spirit within those lines, finding an essential verge in a pitcher perched on the rubber, blinking in for a sign; an infielder smoothing the dirt and glancing up to see what the next pitch will be; and an outfielder taking two hops toward the line late in the game. At the crack of the bat spirit takes wing and plays are made, with applied physics ruling a ball in flight and nine souls flying in pursuit. It's heavenly, and can be hellish.

It's all one spirit. But it plays out in endless variations, some inherently beautiful, others laughable, or damnable. If you're in the game, playing or coaching, it fills you like a deep breath, and can vacate you like a kick in the gut. As a fan, baseball spirit lets you inhabit other souls and bodies, giving you a sense of ownership of the action and a stake in its outcome. If you choose to partake as a fan, the results can also be a mix of heaven and hell, right from the couch. But as a player, the stakes are higher and more literally inspiring. On a patch of ground with bold lines vectoring out to a wide arc of outfield, souls go in motion pursuing a hard white ball in the shape of our planet, only smaller. In spirit, it's immense.

Uniform

Suiting up is where it starts. Pulling on two pair of long socks and a jockstrap. Knocking mud off the spikes. Packing the bat bag with mitts, a scuffed ball, eyeblack, white tape, bug juice, bubblegum and a bottle of water. Gathering the tangible tools and the inner ones that present themselves as a game face. It's a prayer ritual, a meditative reach anticipating the game's effort with relaxed concentration. You put it on. If the day is high blue, the process can be startlingly energizing. And even in cold gray rain, the purpose at its core provides a clear center where visibility is good. The preparatory habits kindle the game's glow and feed it with physical attention.

The goal is to do it the same way every time. The game itself has infinite variations of action and reaction, inexhaustible physics. Playing it — putting it on — is a matter of steady sameness, all the way up from your first unsteady childhood throws to your last sure pitch. The game remains the same as it changes every moment, losing and finding its balance. You try to match its sameness even as you glide through all the changes that life offers up. This effort toward constancy is an act of prayer, an active prayer, willful if never fully conscious.

My hall closet is full of uniforms (from the Latin uniformis, of one form). Parts of them are scattered through drawers and boxes as well. The real keeper is my Gorillas T-shirt, a unique creation, now a ragged green sweat rag; we Gorillas took pride in not having uniforms, everyone finding their own, and beating teams that arrived bedecked in store-bought regalia. Fragments of that non-uniform lie in a heap in the back of the closet, all these years.

I resumed the game in my mid-twenties as a Gorilla, playing fast-pitch softball with guys from the old neighborhood, teammates of mine (some of them) from when I was 6 years old, over State. We reclaimed our formative team, adding more recent pals who'd grown up on other sandlots, and we played three hard and mean seasons in a mud league in Brentwood, Long Island, New York. It was working-class softball — modified fast-pitch with bunting and stealing — played mostly on skin (dirt) infields. A pitching and defense and speed game, it was sometimes brutal, and never a drug-free zone. Those unkempt fields were fringe bazaars for all manner of trade. But whatever singular baggage we had, we brought it to ballplaying battle, coming by train and car, some from the city, others scattered across Long Island, to ride the game ferociously and with all the permission its renegade rules would permit. In twenty years since, there are not many teams I've played on (or against) that could bring the Gorillas down in any sort of ballgame. And none in a brawl.

The closet holds more current uniforms: the proud black Oyster Bay Bombers jersey from my last few seasons playing in Nassau and Suffolk counties; the dark green Columbus Warthogs' with black trim and a big white number 20 on the back from the last few years here in Ohio; the Kenyon staff softball team gray two-button with purple trim, and a purple 20, from the local co-ed softball league. Several black KC workout shirts from my two seasons with the Kenyon College team hang in a row. And in the corner is a gray jersey with a red VILLAGE MARKET across the front — the teenaged Babe Ruth League players I now coach wear it with a Cleveland Indians cap, and are known variously as the Village Market Indians or the Market Dogs. It's all the same uniform, as different as it gets.

The real uniform is underneath. It's the T-shirt you sweat into, two pairs of socks, your jock and wristbands. Finally, it's your skin — the proud flesh afield. It's bone and muscle and connective tissue, as much as you can keep intact. And it's the same every time, never quite uniform.

Catch a Fly Yer Up

Pronounced as a single word — catchaflyerup — with the accent held back for that expectant up (as the hands are held back to hit a ball hard), this was one of those off-field games played whenever brief time and suburban space allowed. Its beauty involved simplicity, a reduction of the game to certain essentials. Blessed by the fact that it could be played with twenty players or two, it was a quickie — could be instantly assembled on Gladstone Avenue after dinner or between other obligations, and played for as long as we had — 'til darkness fell and Dad whistled us in. We'd play catch a fly, you're up on The Dead End and over State and in the street. It was pure.

Catch a fly, you're up has one batter self-hitting — tossing the ball up and lashing long drives— with everyone else in the outfield. If it's only one guy out there, or a couple, they can have their work cut out for them to cover it all. If there's a gang out there, the challenge becomes elbowing off your teammates, all contending for the same sinking liner with arms and hips flying and mitts flashing out to snatch the ball from someone else's glove. The batter hits the ball in the outfielders' general direction, trying to give them a shot at catching it, but not necessarily making it easy. Because as soon as someone catches a fly, he's up, and the batter has to take the field in pursuit of his own fly to regain the at-bat. Catch a fly, you're up occasions a sporting balance and quick symmetry, satisfying the need for a little bit of the game. Its best case features tailing low liners and spectacular rolling catches — do or die, catch a fly, you're up.

What's gained is a slice of the game's moment, its arc. Our mattress fences over State collapsed more than once under the weight of a flying Gladiator putting his Dead End moves to work in a game, catching a fly and getting us all up.

3

GORILLAS

Overpass

The Overpass became a one-on-one stadium in our later youth, when it got harder to recruit 20 kids at a time for a game over State. We didn't consider this then, but the Overpass was a literal extension of State, whose right field hillside carried the elevated parkway across Union Street, the railroad tracks, and a road called Orinoco. We made of it a literal extension of the field and the game, an ideal reduction to the essential pitching-hitting confrontation — a place to inhabit imagination and real ballplaying, all at the same time.

The Overpass was a big concrete bridge spanning a road, the railroad tracks, and another road. It had three huge concrete sections, three pairs of broad parallel walls comprising big tunnels with open ends. The section spanning Union Street was a bit too wide for stickball, and even in those days the traffic on Union was pretty steady. The next section spanned the railroad tracks, and while its measure was better, the tracks and cinders clogged the field. But the Orinoco section was perfect: a less-used, two-lane road 70 feet across from wall to wall, with a 40-foot-high ceiling.

The wall behind the batter was blessed with a painted strike-zone box that served as the more-or-less automatic ump; you pitched into the box for a strike, or missed it for a ball. Outside the box was a less clearly-defined zone for wild pitches, so if a pitch sailed way over a batter's head or behind his back, invisible runners would usually advance.

23

Rosie in the middle distance 1987.

The opposite curb was an ideal pitching rubber. The pitcher had about ten feet behind him to the back wall, and the graffiti there marked automatic zones for hits: this high up a double, this high a triple, over the top of the spray-painted swirls a home run. The ceiling, forty feet up, was an automatic out — and thus the near-homer, the crushed liner that would catch just an inch of the roof before hitting the back wall, provided anguished batters and jubilant pitchers with reason to cuss bitterly or sag with relief.

Grounders fielded cleanly were outs, as were caught fly balls, of course. And strikes were ultimately called by the pitcher, unless the batter looked back quickly enough to see if a pitch hit the box, and pursue an aggrieved (though seldom successful) argument. We gave the pitcher the strike-calling edge, and the hitter reason to go up hacking. It made for great one-on-one competition, with enough of the game's physics intact to make it worth playing every day, sometimes twice.

Nine innings might take an hour or so; it was all pitching and hitting, and dodging the occasional skidding car while fielding a bunt.

With runners on, traffic became strategic. Seeing a car bearing down from either direction, the pitcher would go into a stretch and hold the set. As the car whizzed by he'd throw the pitch — the batter had to catch sight of it through the passing blur. Drivers liked to honk, and the tunnel's booming echoes made hitting all the more challenging under this scenario. It was all fair, and more than once a batter would retaliate by bunting, then dashing for the pitcher's mound in the wake of the passing car. If he reached the pitcher's curb before the pitcher fielded the bunt, he was safe. But the timing on this brought you right to the razor's edge, for if another car was coming from the other direction, you could end up as road kill. No one ever died, but there were a few hard braking incidents that had us fleeing angry drivers. There was also the occasional liner off a car door, which could likewise interrupt a big inning.

Ronnie Fitz was unhittable under the Overpass. Robbie was tough, too. Danny Collins also threw hard stuff off that concrete mound, and others did their best. It was good batting practice, and to this day my Overpass at-bats cough up tactical memories as I twitch in a batter's box somewhere.

But more than that, the Overpass was the real game for us. The play by play was pivotal, and the action riveting. There were occasions when, just at the right moment, after a big grand slam or a key strikeout, a train would come barreling through the adjacent tunnel like the wild sound of a hometown crowd. We'd dance on home plate and wave at its flashing windows, the commuters fleeing the city to spend a passing moment at our ballpark, coloring our game with a blur of real faces and a deafening, glorious roar.

Virtually

Someday I'll build this: take the scale of the Overpass stickball game and wire it up. Engineer an intelligent 1-on-1 baseball court with a strike-zone on one wall wired to register strikes and balls and wild pitches and out throws. The back wall likewise wired with zones to register batted singles, doubles, triples, homers and outs. A plastic indoor mound and tough carpet; good shielded lighting; and Plexiglas walls for spectators in ballpark seating on a courtside incline. Compute the signals to track balls and strikes, hits and outs, and display those on an old-timey scoreboard. Piped-in crowd noise responsive to game situations? It could be done, all of this, with present technology.

What you have is a sanitized and focused version of the Overpass game, sans traffic. A pitcher and batter going 1-on-1, the game reduced perfectly to its essentials. The hit/out zones could be adjusted to handicap one player or the other. And a perfect reduction of 9 innings could be played, as we did, over and over again, in about an hour.

Put several of those courts together — perhaps one larger court for 3-on-3 competition — and you've got a great place for players to hone the game, and for would-be players to compete at any level they can, to act it out and soak it in and be heroes. Hard to imagine something more fun or useful.

Gorillas

The game reclaimed me one Saturday night at East Islip Marina, when I drove up to watch the Gorillas play a C-Division modified fast-pitch softball game on a hardscrabble field by the Great South Bay. I'd just moved back to Long Island after years on the road and a stint in North Carolina, and hadn't played any competitive ball since high school. I ran into Baboon at the grocery store and he urged me to come down to watch them play — Willie, Ty, Danny and others from the Gladstone days. It brought a smile immediately and I promised I'd be there.

When I pulled up to the fence that night and cut the engine in my little Ford, the Gorillas were huddled on the other side, looking disconcerted. They were a man short, with 5 minutes left before a forfeit loss. When they saw me they started waving: jump over the fence and put on this jersey! I was the prodigal player — the long-lost solution to a clear and present problem. We scampered out to the field — they knew to grant me second base — and we played a solid, exciting game, beating a decent team in a pitched battle. I left my feet for two line drives at second, catching them both. It was glory.

The threshold I crossed when I hopped that fence was the game itself, inviting me back in. I felt like I'd never left, and afterwards, sitting in the parking lot after beers, looking out over the deserted field, I smiled right down to my sneakers. I felt my body and soul had come back home.

The best play I ever saw — from the inside — was with the Gorillas in a playoff doubleheader one fine night, two years later. We were coming out of the B Division loser's bracket, and had to beat one tough team to get to the final game with the champs. Both games were on the same field, back to back, so the champs were sitting watching our first game from the stands, sizing up their possible opponents for the final. In a game hard-fought with brilliant and steady defense for both sides, we were up by a run late, but they had runners on with two out. That look swept around the Gorilla infield — on your bellies, knock the ball down, these runners will not score! No way! Next pitch, the batter slashes a wicked bad-hop bounder to Danny Meader at third — the ball knuckling so hard it kicks off the dirt at his feet and takes a high hop off his shin and shoulder, looping high in the air toward short. With the ball in mid-flight, shortstop Stuey flies up off the ground and grabs it bare-handed, slinging a straight-rope throw across his chest to nail the out at first.

The would-be (wouldn't be) champs sagged on the sidelines. Right there, we showed them their time was coming. We blew them off the field in the second game, but that was moot. We had really won both games with that one play.

Uncle Rosie

I have all these nieces and nephews I'm always bragging about, so he calls me Uncle Jerry. I call him Uncle Rosie in return, or sometimes Aunt Rosie. He has an easy laugh and a quick bat, and he now plays centerfield in the over–40 division of the Men's Senior Baseball League. His thick hair is going gray, just a little at a time.

We were teammates for three years with an unforgettable coach named George and a gang of glorious amateurs, wily veterans all. The Stony Brook Cardinals were a pack of aging warriors who gathered every Sunday afternoon to play real baseball on eastern Long Island. Rosie and I shared all the good times the game can bring: we roomed-up on the road in fine resort suites and fleabag rooms in Florida and Arizona; hustled through two-man shag workouts at East Meadow, getting ready for tournaments; and faced the crunch on hot Sundays at our home field at the university and in fog banks of dump gas at Flynn Park in Smithtown on cold autumn nights, with rabid foxes skirting the edges of the light behind us. We had it all, and along with the baseball we had jobs, and loves, and families. But all else falls away on the ballfield, that thick familiar place. Or most of it does.

Rosie's a compact, powerful ballplayer who walks with a graceful stride, bearing a quiet, thoughtful pride. He keeps to himself mostly, until you get to know him; then, a bounding sense of humor emerges, with a bottomless laugh that somehow seems hard-won. His quick eyes come to rest on a middle distance, somewhere between here and there. Come game time, that focus sharpens to matters closer at hand.

He's no longer as quick as he once was, but he gets a great jump on the ball, making up for lost speed with attention and game sense. He has this way of rising to an occasion, and always seems to get there in tough situations. After a hard-fought victory or loss, his demeanor is always the same: outwardly calm, he assesses another game, reliving the at-bats and the turning tides that have spelled a win or a loss. It's all the same to Rosie — no shrieks of joy at winning or excuses for losing. Just quiet eyes measuring the distance between now and then, this pitch or inning or season and the next.

Rosie and I sometimes talk about how we're going to hang them up, but we never do. Springtime comes and we lace up the spikes and go shag flies, and before we know it a season's begun and we're in the thick of it again. Quitting is hard; the game's a familiar habit. We've played for years and years, at home and on the road. I guess we'll always be teammates, even though we've played on different teams more seasons than not.

Rosie's a quick-handed lefty hitter, a slasher. He hits linedrives to all fields, and gets along with teammates in an easy way. But his quietness invariably takes over at odd moments, as he stands looking out over the field. Knowing him as I do, I sometimes wonder what he must be thinking.

He grew up in a working class section of Jersey City and joined the Army out of high school. The American ground war in Vietnam was at its height; like most guys who have seen the worst of wartime, Rosie's life has an interregnum that he doesn't much talk about. He was one of the lucky ones; upon recovering from his wounds he got some just desserts. Rosie played Army baseball during the 1972 and 1973 seasons in Europe, traveling with his unit to ballgames in Germany, Spain, Italy, Belgium and Holland. "It was like going from hell to heaven — just like that," he once told me. As he got stronger and played better, he put away what was lost and experienced a sense of rebirth that survivors sometimes find. But the losses came back in his sleep, and on long nights without. When waking brought back the real opportunity, he played with all the life-energy he'd been spared.

Now, three decades down the road, he stands in the on-deck circle twirling a bat and staring out at the diamond, his eyes patrolling slowly from right field to left. When we room together on these trips, he'll awake in the middle of the night in a sweat and walk around the room, looking for a way out in the dark. In the morning when I awake he'll be up, sitting quietly in his stirrups and sliding pads, gazing out at the parking lot. Come game time he's his usual self, stroking singles, running down liners in the gaps, and joking in the on-deck circle. And then, as sudden as death, he goes silent. He's contemplating his next at-bat, or reliving his last one. Or thinking about other stuff.

Goldy

Rosie and Goldy are bookends. They're both New York specimens: working guys, wise-cracking guys, ballplayers. And they're both Vietnam-era vets. But while Ron Rosenberg was diving in and out of hot jungles, Ron Goldman was boogying with blondes in Iceland courtesy of the U.S. Navy. That's so Goldy. He has a lucky streak a mile wide, all of his own making. Goldy's act is a lot more glamorous than Rosie's, his personality a quick-witted friendly gab that catches peoples' attention like a river catches sunlight. With his handsome diamond smile, Goldy can talk to anyone and make him laugh. With all the hardships of any adult life, his is played on the upbeat. He's the same way at third base.

A step and a dive, is how Goldy describes playing third. It's all positioning, and it's all feet, where you're standing. He measures each batter and situation knowingly, having played on all sorts of empty lots and asphalt schoolyards. It's what the field will give you, the spot where a certain batter will hit a ball hard, and how you get to that spot. You have no time to think at third — you can only react. A hard ball right at you is easy; no time for fear. You just have to stay down, is all. No matter how that ball is blistered, you stay down on it or it eats you up.

To either side, it's a step and a dive. Goldy plays the line that way, usually, unless he's fading toward the hole for a lefty. Late in the game he'll protect it more, a half-step and a dive. He plays shallow like old Oliver "The Ghost" Marcelle, the great Negro Leaguer. He's always moving with the pitch, crouching his frame low toward the plate as the pitcher releases the ball. He keeps his eyes low, the better to stay on the ball. With fine timing he finds poise at a balanced moment with the swing, timing off the batter more than off the pitcher. His concentration gives him an edge, and his play at third is glorious to watch. He has the sharp looseness of a great third baseman, and has saved many an inning with great good humor, a step and a dive.

By George

Rosie and I were walking up the ramp to the loge level at Shea, moving toward that glorious green light at the end of the tunnel where the field opens before you like a bright, unexpected meadow. The place had an early pregame pulse, an eager crowd clustered in the rail seats and the scattered along the upper levels. Like us, they'd come out to watch batting practice, to gawk and ponder and speculate.

We were chuckling about a character we'd just seen on the train. It seemed we saw him on every trip to Shea — a big, bouncy middle-aged guy who moved like a big/little kid, up on the balls of his feet, excited to be heading to the ballpark again. We were comparing him to some character we'd both seen in the movies — an eternal boy — when we crested the top of the Shea tunnel and stopped to gaze out at the St. Louis Cardinals dotted across the field, taking grounders and batting practice.

The cage was jammed with hitters waiting their turn for a quick "two and out" hitting drill. Screens stood in front of first and second, and the Redbirds were hopping around in small circles, shagging and throwing and styling. You sweep your eyes across a pregame field like that to see an endless variety of postures and polish, the Big Game rehearsed as a daily job, then played for real, and then again tomorrow. From our fan perspective, these routines glimmer. We were dazzled by it. But Tinkerbell really gonged us hard as we both fixed our eyes on the mound, where the BP pitcher was an older guy with the number 3 on his back.

It was George! For a moment, it truly was, and we were astonished. This guy was looking and throwing just like George Altemose, our coach and DH from the Stony Brook Cardinals. He was winding up the same way, throwing straight fastballs and ducking behind the L-screen as line drives came crackling by. We could actually believe the sight of him there—throwing BP to the St. Louis Cardinals at Shea. We shook our heads. It is George. No, we looked again, it isn't him. But the guy could be his twin.

For George, coaching our amateur team was what he endured for a sure spot in the lineup. He agonized over ministrations of the defense and pitching staff, all the second-guessing and arguments he got from a roster of 30-plus-year-olds, most of whom had played for years and coached as well. But George kept the steady grip on the till so that he could get his swings—the object of his devotion. George always batted himself third in the order, and wore number 3 on his uniform. Like Babe Ruth, only it was a Cardinal jersey, and an amateur one at that. At our Saturday practices and Sunday games, George always took enormous swings, and when he connected the ball would disappear into the sky. He'd trot around the bases stiff-legged, like the Babe, and wait until he was back in the dugout to let a bright smile light up his face. When he hit a grounder, he was an easy out; a shortstop could juggle the ball, drop it, kick it, step on it, drop it again, and still throw George out. Speed was not his game. He was all power.

We used to joke that George had lineup cards with his name preprinted in the three hole. No matter how he or the team was going, hot or cold, rain or shine, George would bat there, always expecting some kid to try to sling a fastball by him. He'd flinch at breaking balls, and lunge at changeups; but throw him a fastball and he'd take you to school. The pitcher's head would jerk around to watch that fastball on its way out of town, with George doing his little trot out of the box, face impassive, touching them all before striding back into the dugout to reward himself, and us, with a beaming Babe Ruth grin.

♦

When Rosie and I came to the Cardinals in 1985, the team was languishing at the bottom of the fall Stan Musial League and George was looking for players to build a winning campaign in the newly-forming Men's Senior Baseball League, the brainchild of a fellow pickup-game player with a plan. The MSBL today comprises hundreds of leagues around the U.S. and abroad, and provides a solid context of organized amateur baseball in divisions defined by age: under-thirty, over-thirty, over-forty, and so on. In the MSBL's fledgling season of 1986, four teams from Long Island competed in a more-or-less organized fashion for a full summer, and the Cardinals won the first MSBL championship, a fact the league now officially discounts as "pre–MSBL." No matter. I was on the mound for that win, in the final inning, after a succession of Cardinal pitchers had blown a nine-run lead by walking a conga line. With darkness bearing down and the tying run on third — two outs — Goldy caught my eye from the bag as the distracted runner took a short lead off the bag and turned to listen to chatter from his dugout, and we picked him clean. With a two-foot lead, he never even leaned back toward the bag until Goldy tapped him on the shoulder to tag him out. Of such moments are championships made in Little Leagues and Big Little Leagues. I staggered off the mound (having walked in several runs myself, struggling to throw a strike to this batter blinking at me through the gloaming); in a suitable gesture, George's young daughter scampered onto the field and, shrieking, pied me in the face with a fistful of confetti.

Champions of what, exactly, we were unsure. But we'd staggered across that finish line as a team, and in coming seasons, as the league got better, we did too. We were always there in the playoffs in those early MSBL seasons as the league grew from four to seventeen to over a hundred teams, then went national.

The Stony Brook Cardinals were a flashy bunch. A few had played in the pro minors, and most had played college ball or army ball. Rosie roamed center field and I had second base, with Goldy flashing gold at third. Dominic Melillo was one of our kid studs—now barely thirty, he'd played shortstop at Villanova eight or nine years back, and was in great shape—a fluid glider with quick sure hands. Jimmy Fogarty had first base, he of the Boston minors twenty years back and Otis Elevator ever since. Behind the dish, Bob Margolin personified courage as a catcher—a bear of a guy with a degenerative spinal condition who nonetheless would grind it out every Sunday behind the plate, a solid wall at his crucial spot. Bob was the clear conscience of the Cardinals, his gentleness built upon a rare kind of competitive will and strength, and always, great good humor.

The Cardinal pitching staff was an assortment, to say the least. It featured Al Poxon, a big, slow happy lefty who'd spent some time in the Pirates' minors, and Len Tartamella, a trial lawyer and ambidextrous pitcher who liked to baffle the opposition by quietly switching arms in the middle of a game. He threw just the same from either side, and more than once we watched teams argue in their dugout over whether he'd been throwing lefty (or righty) the whole game. George was always on the lookout for new talent, and he picked up a young attorney named Chris Kent ("Superman" to us) who threw hard low stuff and brought his tough litigious fire to the mound.

After the MSBL season ended each September, George would reconstitute a team for a quick snowflake season in October and into November, in the fall Stan Musial League. He'd add some young legs for this 18-and-over campaign of twenty or so games, where we'd watch umpires literally crying from the cold on blustery weeknights under spare lights and biting sleet.

Through most of these seasons we had the university field at Stony Brook as a home base for the Sunday afternoon games, switching to lighted Smithtown parks for midweek night games. We were very much at home anywhere, as long as it was a ballyard. The Cardinals competed in national MSBL tournaments in Arizona and Florida, whooping it up in the autumn warmth of Tempe and Tucson and Tallahassee, sprinting across deserted minor league ballparks as if we owned the very core of the baseball universe. There was little else going on in the world when we played, and whatever was, you couldn't prove it by us. It was just the game, this one and the next, and those who danced it beside you.

Dash

Her hair was long and straight, fine and full, parted clean down the middle with discernible strands of reddish-brown from her German-American father and a rich black shine from her Japanese mother. Her eyes were sparkling brown almonds, and her lips had natural dark edges that negated any need for makeup. She wore none. Her skin was the color of tea with cream and a bit of honey. Smart and mischievous, she wore bluejeans and man-tailored work shirts and well-worn running shoes. Nothing could mask her sheer feminine strength, small and full of power. She'd be impossibly sexy in anything — overalls or a bikini or a baseball uniform. So falling in love with her was like falling off a boat and hitting water. It was pure, inevitable, and startling in the best way. And all that follows is colored with love, even now, years after a medieval November when love walked away.

Susan was a beautiful athlete and an exquisite ballplayer. She crossed baseball's treacherous gender line with great dignity, amid all sorts of risk — a small young nisei with great talent and surpassing determination. This graceful Amerasian girl could run like a thoroughbred across the outfield with her ponytail flying, then jog in with a faint sly smile and a ball in her glove to goosebump the boys on the bench.

I met her across a desk at a small software company on Long Island. She was interviewing me for a tech-writing job — one of my first, over twenty years ago. The office was new, sleek and modern, with high butcher-block desks and soft lighting. She was frank and funny, and the formalities of the interview soon dissolved into an easy rapport. We sat close and talked with plain good humor. The job she described — stirring her tea while I sipped mine — was just what I'd been looking for: a small startup company, young and energetic, with a plan and some backing. They'd begun a year before writing Pascal code on computers arranged around a Ping-Pong table in the boss' basement. After selling the rights to their first software program to Apple Computer for their Apple II systems, now the young programmers were developing follow-up products they'd market themselves. I listened, gazing at a spot just below her lip, feeling sentimental for what hadn't happened yet.

She eyed me back with a slender smile and a semi-tough blush. It was like meeting myself in someone else, a long-lost twin, only better. Gifted and sharp and beautiful, she seemed to like me as immediately as I liked her. She hired me, and we went to work.

Over the course of that first year on the job we worked hard — all of us did — and she and I shared countless hours writing specs, designing screens, and testing software for bugs. And many long nights as well, with Neil Young whining on the boom box and a hush of young intelligence earnestly working all around us. We were a bunch of night-owls; the village police would tap on the windows at 3 or 4 in the morning to check in on us. We kept sleeping bags under our desks, but didn't use them much; if we were there, we were working — in a comfortable flow of productive thought.

As our friendship grew, love and work and play intertwined through each day and into each night. We'd sit up late at the high tables listening to Neil, not wanting to leave work, the tea steaming up with traces of Asian hillsides. Those nights brought to life a silent language full of physical nuance — shoulders at rest, souls flowing out, our eyes in a slow dance around expressive tokens. She'd swing her hair and smile, then shift into her best foggy Neil imitation, strumming and singing along in a cracked falsetto. I'd jiggle laughing, or simply sit still, staring wide-eyed with wonder at her small perfections.

I was oblivious, when we first met, to her athletic achievements. As I came to know more of what she'd already accomplished (barely in her twenties) my respect deepened. She came to watch my Gorilla ballgames, impressed with a brand of softball she'd never seen before — fast-pitch with bunting and stealing and great defense and fistfights, working-class white and hispanic teams with lots of fire. Some of the Gorillas knew about her racewalking exploits from the newspapers. They had a respectful regard for her as she looked on astonished at the muddy, gritty but graceful Gorilla play. I don't think we ever lost when she was on the sidelines.

She'd always been the tiny tomboy, eager to challenge boys at anything athletic. At age eight she owned the best baseball bat on her block, thus assuring herself of participation in twilight suburban street games. She was a slash linedrive hitter and the fastest runner by far. It was easy for the boys to accept her; she met them more than halfway athletically.

Harder for her were the occasional exclusions from other boy stuff as time went by, and the baleful look her mother would give when she'd beg to join them in the street for some swings after dinner. She won her way into the street games with the sheer torque of her desire — an irresistible force, tiny and driven like a piston. On other occasions — family gatherings and the quotidian routines of home — she was the dutiful daughter in the Japanese mode, a slight quiet shadow, content to spend hours alone with books or baseball cards. She could clear a dinner table like a silent breeze, and wash a load of dishes without making a sound. But put her near a ballgame and she'd charge in like a wild pony, eager to flex and show her best.

In high school she joined the boys' cross-country track team (there being none for girls) and fast became a team leader. Her coach nicknamed her Dash. Standing five-foot tall with an 80-pound frame, her endurance seemed to have no limit. She ran everywhere she went. Three miles to school on a solid run door to desk, then home for lunch, then back again, then track practice. The coach had a different runner lead the pack for each day's workout, and her turns inspired frightful awe among the lanky boys. She'd lead a wary line of them out for the worst of Long Island's north shore hills, finding tougher and tougher roadside courses of 12 to 15 miles. The boys were not amused. But she held and treasured their respect, and her joking banter made it hard to stay mad at her. They loved the sight of her long hair swinging up ahead, even as they struggled to catch up.

Cross-country meets were held near the shore, on wooded trails traversing a steep moraine called Cardiac Hill. Coming down that hill on a dead run one afternoon, she hit loose gravel and fell hard, tearing cartilage in her ribcage. A most painful injury, it was her first real debilitating hurt, and she took it hard. Enduring weeks of every move hurting, she finally started running again. But while she gradually built up her distance, her speed was not what it had been. The twisting torso movement wasn't so bad, but the pounding of the run brought her to a pained and frustrated stop time and again. She was at a loss, and wept often when alone. She missed the adrenaline feed, the rush of leading the pack up another hill. She was not herself, and it darkened her like low clouds.

Her track coach finally introduced her to a local university coach involved in racewalking. This peculiar track event, long popular in

Europe, China and South America, remains a curiosity in America. It manifests in crowds of colorful walkers doing long road courses, with competitors sustaining speeds over marathon distances to rival the times of strong amateur runners. Racewalking demands a strict form — no matter how fast a walker is walking, they can never break into a run: one foot must always be touching the ground, and each leg has to straighten fully at the knee with each stride. Sanctioned races are watched carefully by judges, who disqualify walkers for breaking these rules of form.

Racewalkers wiggle along with exaggerated hip thrusts, some more gracefully than others. Suz was a natural. The attentive coach guided her first racing sprints, shaping her natural ability into a streamlined effort. She had little of the familiar rib pain, absent the pounding of the run, and she quickly developed a fast-gliding, fluid form. In her first scholastic competition she set a new state record, coming out of nowhere to burst to the front of a competitive bracket. Suddenly, this new sport offered amazing opportunities. She flew to California for nationals, and finished second. Back in New York she won the first medal ever awarded at the Empire State Games in 1978. Despite the fact that the women's walk was not yet an Olympic event, she was invited to fly aboard Air Force One to Greece to receive the Olympic flame two weeks before the Lake Placid Winter Olympics in 1980. Mingling with diplomats, generals and journalists, she even bit the bullet and wore a gown for the formal dinners. She'd come a long way in a short time, and felt incandescent and somewhat bewildered. But she carried herself with the kind of friendly nonchalance that could grace any room and any company.

The competitions continued. She walked for the U.S. National Team in Mexico, Norway, and China, holding her place among the top three American walkers. At the first Goodwill Games in Moscow she walked a strong race, then found herself in a rowdy group of U.S. sprinters and hurdlers shooting 4th of July bottle rockets out the hotel window, squealing as Soviet soldiers scattered across Red Square. On the flight home, when their "Aeroflop" flight cleared Soviet airspace they broke into a lusty American cheer — on top of the world.

All this time we grew closer and more comfortable in each other's company — her returns from trips abroad always aglow with a sense of triumphant homecoming. She spent one birthday competing in Italy, and I wired an order for flowers, not knowing that 100 dollars American would fill the tiny hotel lobby with an embarrassing truckload of them.

When she walked in the 1984 Olympic Trials in Los Angeles, I tuned in the TV in New York to watch the coverage, which began just as her race was scheduled to go off. With the commentator carrying on about the meet's headliners—the star sprinters and hurdlers—little legs racewalked behind him on the far side of the track, across the very top of the screen. I got down on my hands and knees in front of the TV and tried to look up those legs to spot her, but to no avail. The 20k walk went off while taped highlights of other events played. She finished third, which would have qualified her for the U.S. Olympic Team if the women's walk had been included, but it wasn't, yet. Joan Benoit won the first women's marathon during those Olympics; other distance events for women would have to wait for the doddering International Olympic Committee to catch up with the women's rights movement. Suz peaked too soon for an Olympiad—that ultimate amateur competitive opportunity—through no fault of her own. She was ready, even if others were not.

But then, through happenstance, amateur baseball proved ready for her. I had graduated from Gorilla softball to Stony Brook Cardinal baseball, and in between track meets she'd been showing up at our practices with her mitt and spikes, shagging flies during interminable batting practices. George took note of her speed and adequate arm in the outfield, while various Cardinals challenged her to basepath races and never beat her. Finally, one autumn evening, the inevitable happened. A *Newsday* sports writer described it under this patronizing headline in October 1986:

A Little Lady Who Plays Hardball

When Sue Liers accompanied Jerry Kelly to a Stan Musial League game earlier this fall, the last thing she expected to do was put on a uniform and participate. With only eight players and forfeit time approaching, Stony Brook Cardinal manager George Altemose turned to Liers and asked her to suit up. She eagerly obliged and thus became the first woman to play baseball at the Stan Musial level on Long Island.

Her effect on the game may not have been as significant as teammate Rob Marto's 15 strikeouts, but without her there would have been no game. "We were a man short. If I wasn't there they wouldn't have been able to play," said Liers. "The guys were happy I played. But the opposing players felt uncomfortable, I think."

To Altemose, it was the only alternative. Now Liers regularly attends Cardinal games, not as a spectator but as a roster player. "She can run real well and does a decent job in the outfield," said Altemose. "She gives 100 percent and is working on her hitting."

A 27-year-old computer science graduate of Stony Brook University, she took the field that misty September evening at Sawyer Park in West Babylon knowing not to expect to be a world-beater. "I wanted to do my best," said Liers, who has played softball for 19 years. "I know the basics but baseball is a lot harder than softball."

Her presence enabled the Cardinals to pull out a 4-3 victory. "I knew we'd be short players at times and I'd asked her what she thought about playing," said Kelly. "She was excited about it but her parents weren't too wild about the idea. Her father's concerned about her safety, and also the implications for her racewalking career."

As a racewalker, Liers has been successful since the 10th grade. She is a member of the United States National Track & Field team and placed third in the National Championships in June in Eugene, Ore. Conscious of injury that could affect her racewalking, she wears wrestling pads to protect her knees. "The pads are to prevent injury," said Liers. "Baseball is fun but racewalking is serious business."

Her string of racewalking victories includes a national indoor title at Madison Square Garden in February of 1981 and appearances in four National Championships.

In her first at-bat for the Cardinals, she walked, stole second and went to third on an overthrow. "Her second time up I threw inside and tried to intimidate her," said opposing pitcher Mike Kozyrski of the Pirates. "But give her credit, she hung in there." Liers worked the count to 2–2 and grounded out to first. In her final at-bat she struck out.

The following Sunday morning at Murphy Junior High School in Stony Brook, Liers pinch-ran for the 43-year old Altemose. With the 5-foot, 100-pounder on second base, the next batter lofted a fly ball to rightfield. When the ball was caught she tagged up and raced to third, challenging the arm of the Pirates' Bobby Graham. "I never expected her to go," said Graham. "It jolted my pride and ego when she tagged safely." Graham, who later took the mound and struck out Liers in the seventh inning, said, "I was determined to strike her out. I needed something to regain a little self-esteem. She's earned the respect of all players on the field."

"Batting was difficult at first, because I was afraid I wouldn't see the ball well enough to get out of the way of a wild pitch," said Liers, who wears glasses. "I've always wanted to play baseball. Now I'm finding out what it's like to play the game. Winning at any level feels great, and this level of this game is a new challenge for me."

The Fall Stan Musial League offers players the chance to enjoy the season a little longer. Some college and high school players are here to seriously sharpen skills for the upcoming spring season, to get in more swings and more innings, but most of these players sacrifice football Sundays, family outings and leaf cleanup to enjoy the beautiful fall weather and a twinbill. For Sue Liers, it's an experience she'll always remember.

Gregg Sarra © 1986, Newsday Inc. Reprinted with permission.

♦

We protected Suz as best we could — but she needed little, really. Her at-bats had everyone watching, and our pitchers would retaliate quickly if she was hit by a pitch. But this wasn't really a fighting league like the Gorillas had played in, and she didn't catch much flack. She played left field like a demon — shallow, daring batters to hit it over her head — and caught everything she could get to. Her bouncing leads from first rattled pitchers and infielders alike, and the blur of her pumping arms and legs never failed to get the dugout to its feet cheering as she rounded third, heading for home.

♦

Time traveled, and we settled into familiar patterns of work and play. Our company lost momentum, tripped up by a single bad management decision, and after working for weeks without pay, we finally gave up the ghost. A large software company swallowed us up and put us to work on bigger systems, but it wasn't the same — no more late nights programming to Neil Young, no sweet romance of the uphill battle. We were reduced to showing up and getting caught in circular projects. I left the company after a year, hungry for the focus of another start-up. She stayed on, and our orbits began to degrade.

Around that time my father retired after 34 years at the same blue-collar job, and then took sick. After weeks of pain and failing appetite we finally prevailed upon him to see the doctor, and his thinly-shrouded fears proved out. The diagnosis was bone cancer, with six months to live. We brought home a broken soul. He made us promise not to put him back in the hospital — "I just want to be here, home" — and we held to our word. I drove him to his daily chemo sessions, and then to the boat basin to watch the churning water. Day in day out, we'd sit in the car and he'd sneak a smoke, gazing out at the bay. He was not much for deep talk, but we'd look for harbor seals and speculate on the weather, the big shoreline sky never failing to offer up cause for wonder. Silently, we inched closer than we'd ever been — sometimes literally leaning on each other without comment. I lived in a shroud of his pain and when the time came, I learned how to shoot him up with morphine. I hated giving him those needles, dulling pain with pain. He wasted fast, shrinking in the big bed, my little father. Those weeks, I walked as though up to my knees in snow, slowed down by a gravity I'd never felt. My own orbit degraded to a silent spin, putting out pulses of quiet radioactive anger. She stayed away from me, and I kept her away from my muddled fears and regrets. There was no one to reach but my fading father, and he was barely reachable.

Late one night the phone rang, and it was my mother sobbing "He's gone." I wept myself dry in the shower while Susan slept in the next room, then drove home to his bedside, finding him curled up in death's stillness, his mouth open, life gone. Stroking his head, I felt such sadness as I can hardly express. Even with all this time to prepare, I wasn't ready for him to be gone. I wondered how people cope when they lose someone suddenly — the shock of it. I sat with my mother and tried to answer her emptiness, but for a time, could only offer more of my own to anyone who cared to listen to the silence.

It was a hard time — had been for months — and in my funk I'd lost sight of Susan. Walking my father toward the finish line had taken all I had, emotionally, and without intention I cut her off, turning inward to attend to my own hurt. She retreated into her doting family, and they sheltered her from my shadow. We spent more and more time apart. Our love never turned to hate, or anything like that; but it died as my father was dying, and she answered my neglect by leaving me.

Two weeks after the funeral, she moved out. I was a sad heap, and would spend a year mourning all such loss, staring at the bay or sleep-walking alone in the sunlight. Baseball was all that relieved me, and I played for no one but those no longer there.

Now, ten years later, I've long since picked up those pieces. But some of the whole is truly gone, and what was no longer is. I call Suz on her birthdays and we share easy talk, comfortable, respectful. She has a boy of her own now, and a good husband whose attentions are steadfast and firm. The forlorn house is long gone, but we keep what we earned with each other and save it as a keeper.

Emotion in motion endures. I do, at odd moments, look out into left field expecting to see her dash for the gap and make a graceful catch, then smirk as she hops into the dugout. She stays with me that way, her black hair swinging from behind.

Yanquis

In my last year with the Cardinals—the team getting old and start-ing to lose with disconsolate regularity—I was approached by a local Hispanic team looking for a second baseman. The Brentwood Yanquis were trying to build a winner, and frankly would have preferred another Puerto Rican in my place, but they added a few of us gringos to try to put them over the top. I played two seasons for them, and we were always knocking on the door in the county finals, though we never quite won it all. Our games were glorious, hard-fought affairs played under the critical eyes of their wives and girlfriends and mothers, who showed up regularly and never hesitated to berate our errors or cheer hard and loud for our rallies. I learned a lot of Spanish from them, none of which I'll repeat here. Suffice it to say they were real New York fans, with kindred blood boiling.

Rob Santiago and his brother Richie anchored the squad — Roberto on the mound, Ricardo catching — and the rest of the infield was gov-erned by a bunch of true warriors, some of them cops from an East New York, Brooklyn precinct. The sight of handguns in the dugout never filled me with cheer, but these guys were devoted ballplayers first and always, and when fistfights erupted (spurred at times by racial slur) a bloody nose was just a price to pay for standing up to some redneck. Nothing would back these guys down, guns or no guns. They talked a lot of happy trash and played with a certain style, always ready to get down in the dirt to pluck out a win, then strut the victory. I was proud to be among them, if never completely of them. There was nothing quite like belting a two-run double for those mad mamacitas on the sidelines.

4

BOMBERS

Ty

Ty Cobb, whose mother shotgunned his father's head clean off, said it this way: "Baseball is something like a war." He certainly played it that way, sharpening his legendary spikes and wanting nothing more than to beat the bastards today and have another whack at them tomorrow. Or was he that way? Was he really all fire and sulphury soul, pursued by demons? Or was it more that he was guided by one true urgency: to be the best at this so-called game — its most expert player — and not come home a failure. Or not come home at all.

Ty Cobb's long-gone dead, but his soul afire comes back to visit the living, most often in children, believe it or not. Kids find that demon-seed desire and partake of it without shame or the means to source it, or the need. They're children, after all, and we protect them to some extent from their own deeds. If worse comes to worse, we lock them up 'til they're eighteen then set them free.

Willie Walsh was the closest soul I ever knew to that of old Ty, from our Gladstone Gladiator boyhood days right through to Gorilla glory. He kept his kindness well hidden, and there was some, but his self and body drove relentlessly hard-outward in any contest with fierce abandon and no quit. Willie would fight anyone, despite the fact that he stood 5 foot 9 and weighed in at maybe 170. The hardest puncher around, he'd jump up in someone's face with no hesitation, sometimes just to stir things up. He'd go for the biggest guy and flatten him quick,

Bomber brain-trust: Joe, Paulie, Charlie & Wilbur, 1994.

hard enough to give him pause about getting back up. Of course, there were times when Willie'd get flattened, battered in fact, but he didn't seem to fear that and never shied away from its possibility.

All of that Ty soul rides at the top of Willie's game, but it also has a bottom: a deep and very funny sense of the absurd, of life's limits just there to be tested, and an intelligent sense of the poetic. He's managed to walk a fine line for many years now, could easily have wound up in jail, but he found ways to get out of trouble before being consumed by it, almost as if his self-drive refused to grant the law its quarter. He found ways to win. Willie was one of those ultimate comrades — you wanted to be on his team, on his side, not up against him. We witnessed his blood rage more than many times put up against an opponent, but as his teammates we also basked in his humor, his way with words and his mound antics — unbowed before anything, never embarrassed.

Willie was accompanied, always, by his gentle younger brother. Michael Walsh was the softest-speaking guy you could ever find. He was compact like Willie, but with broader shoulders and greater strength, and this shy, quiet demeanor. More than quiet, it was like a radiance — you could ask anyone who knew him, Michael shone. He had that Buddha quality, a celestial intensity right in his moment.

They were both fine ballplayers, but where Willie was a go-go demon, all combustible hustle, Michael was on a fine glide. He had all the quiet grace Willie lacked, and they balanced each other metaphysically. But also physically. Because Michael also had the steel, only more polished and shrouded. I remember Willie picking a fight one night in a Gorilla game — Baboon was pitching, Willie was catching and jawing at this big galoot of a guy from the other team. The galoot took umbrage, dropped his bat and began taking swings at bob-and-weave Willie. Michael comes charging in from center field on a dead run and blindside tackles the guy, putting him right into the chain-link fence. His team took a step back, recoiling at the sheer violence. The fighting part was over.

It was not wise to mess with Willie when his little brother was around. Gentle as he was, Michael would join Willie's chaos in an instant and settle matters brutally. Afterwards, in the dugout, he'd smile his shy grin and look a little sheepish. We called him Ty.

Leadoff

Let's take it back a bit: That March week in 1987 that Rosie and I spent at Vin Pica's Coast Baseball School in Fort Pierce, Florida — eating baloney sandwiches and feeding on fastballs. Slanting sun and relentless wind is what I remember, and those gaping high-school kids who thought we were pros and were scared to talk to us at that first night's dinner. Vin herded us all through hours of scrimmages and drills, and a lot of time in the cage breaking down hitting mechanics and building them back his way. He promised we'd see our averages rise 100 points if we were faithful to his system. And we still have his seven steps tattooed in memory:

1. Assume a comfortable stance
2. Open it up a little
3. Front shoulder down

4. Arms away from body

5. Bat back and still

6. Watch the pitcher's hand

7. When he shows you his butt, show him yours.

We went through that checklist for every season, every time we stepped in the box. You take your place; it's yours to take. You occupy the box and try to own the space beside it, over the plate. The seven steps serve to settle, rehearse and focus you to the task of hitting a hard pitch harder. All of your parts — legs, shoulders, arms, hands, butt and eyes — get set to stay on the pitch and uncoil through a sure, quick swing. Finally, it's the eyes and hands that hit, and if the rest of you can torque it up at just the right moment, as bat finds ball, then you'll drive it hard somewhere.

As it turned out, Vin was right. His system did add a hundred points to our averages. Rosie and I went back and forth reminding each other for years, pulling out of slumps and catching fire with Vin's seven steps.

But that's just mechanics. The fabric of the game lies somewhere within those adjustments. It unfolds with your instinctive twitch at the ping of the bat, the feel of the ball on the bat head for just that instant that you turn it around and let it rip.

Cutoff

Most vivid are those throws from outfielders — with runners going, a possible play at third or at the plate — moments that seem to slow as the ball arcs in.

As the cutoff man your hands are up, and as the throw nears you turn sideways and reach for it. Quick transfer is everything — catching, grabbing and firing a strike, all in one motion, using your legs. Kind of like turning two at second, only the ball's not turning a corner, but passing directly through you and hitting the after-burners via your hips. Those bang-bang plays bring it all together — outfield-throw-relay-strike-tag-out. Quicker than you can say it, the worm turns.

It's all about grabbing momentum and putting it where it needs to be. Failing that, the run scores or runners move up, and the pitcher sweats, and the infield draws in and tries to recollect. You make that throw and you turn the tide; you fail and the sea pours in through a big hole in the hull, and the ship sinks, and your beloved teammates drown in loser's hell. That's all.

Bombers

I spent my last three years in New York playing second base for the Oyster Bay Bombers and a host of black ancestors. The original Bombers were a Negro semi-pro team in the 1940s and '50s. Their centerfielder, Paulie Collins, was our patron saint and third base coach. He spun tales of that talented Bomber squad playing 60 games one season with but a single loss, and his old teammates came down to cheer for us scruffy white boys, graceful black gentlemen in their best Sunday suits flashing gold-tooth smiles as they scattered stories about beating Whitey Ford when he was a young amateur from Queens, and playing before big crowds there in Oyster Bay Village on hot Sunday afternoons in postwar glory days. Their fluid strut defied disbelief, even as they colored everything rosy.

The new Oyster Bay Bombers featured Paulie in the third-base coaching box and Charlie Moore, a gruff but gracious ex–motorcycle cop, managing stoically on the sidelines. His son Chuck played shortstop and was our closer, nailing down one victory after another with hard ninth-inning heat. Other pitchers included the hot-headed Sal Tavernese, a handsome Italian kid with a cross-eyed temper. Another Italian — a northerner in contrast to Sicilian Sal — was our lefty junkballer Joe Rizli, who wore a sort of goofy expression with his cap tilted to one side, but who could shut down fastball hitters with a mix of slow southpaw stuff. Tod Hafner was our speed demon centerfielder and leadoff hitter. Tod was an amateur who clearly took one part of his game to a professional level. "Half-nut" was the best defensive centerfielder I ever played with — he could go back on balls with the very best of them. He'd creep in shallow and charge to cut off anything hit to short center, getting a great jump to snag a dying quail or a hard line shot at his shoe-tops. But better yet, anything blasted hard and deep had to outrace him, and not many flyballs could. His ability to read the ball off the bat was so fine that he could turn and sprint full-speed, with nary a glance back until his instincts brought him to the very spot the ball would land. He was usually there waiting, but could also snare a deep fly in either gap on a full-tilt boogie run.

Joe Arena was our enforcer at the plate, a delivery-truck driver and compulsive cage hitter who spent countless hours at batting cages all over the New York metropolitan area. Joe was a hitting machine, always our biggest threat. His pal Billy ("Wilbur") Charlock was a great catcher with bad knees, another clutch performer and willing fighter, taking shit from no one. As a group, the Bombers came to battle like the Gorillas; we brought lots of attitude and purpose to the game. No matter what, we were seldom really out of one. Even if Sal was wild and we spotted them a bunch of runs early, we came back swinging. Our best games saw strong pitching, cool defense, clutch hitting and smart baserunning flow together in magnificent harmony, making our black ancestors' gold shine bright.

My last game with the Bombers in 1994 ended with Joe Arena's liner to left, and the impossible catch by that ringer leftfielder. It was a playoff game at Bay Park, a windy field with the bay howling beyond the left field trees. We were down to nine guys after an early altercation at the plate, with two of ours and two of theirs tossed for brawling. In the sixth inning I slide into secondbase hard on a busted sacrifice bunt, miss the baseman and hit the bag, hard plastic anchored in a steel sleeve. The old ankle pops, and I'm seeing stars. Their third baseman comes over and says he heard it pop from way over there. They drag me back to the dugout where Charlie does a fine job of taping it up, old football coach that he is; I go back out to play third and nail two guys laying down bunts.

Adrenaline works its wonders through the game, and through the bigger brawl afterwards, started by the Puerto Rican girlfriends. Two of them jumped one of our Bomberettes, who misguidedly wandered over to their side right after that final catch to give them shit about running their mouths the whole game and calling us maricons— queers. The two chicas start pummeling her, and Carlos the Weasel scampers out of their dugout and bashes her in the head with a full can of Coke, opening a nasty gash at her hairline. One of our guys jumps him, then several of theirs, then all of both, in a melee right there on the concrete behind their dugout. Shoves and fists at first, then Carlos picks up a bat, and we surround him shouting to put it down or we'll take it away and beat you with it. He looks around — the ringers had hastily departed when the fighting broke out — hell, they'd done their work — and his pause is long enough to break the spell. The riot immediately drops a notch to screaming insults and bold posturing. Four squad cars arrive, then a couple of ambulances, but the only dust-off is the dazed Bomberette with the bloody head. The cops refuse to arrest Carlos, because everybody's story is different, and his victim can't pick him out of a back-of-the-ambulance lineup (her eyes still swirling). Charlie protests the game, and it turns out Carlos had five nonroster players there, including the pitcher, catcher, shortstop and two outfielders. The win is nulled and we move on to the next round of playoffs. But I'm done for that season. I head off to tryouts for the Kenyon College Lords two weeks later with a floppy ankle, eager to rehab it again and play some gentlemanly college baseball. Little did I know.

Game Days

Will-to-win is decisive in amateur ball. The sheer physical play isn't nearly as consistent as in the bigs, and mistakes are made. Recovery play — picking up the pieces after a couple of errors or poor pitches — makes all the difference at amateur levels. This ability to recover game flow is so clearly driven by the heart and mind in tandem, the courage to stay loose and keen, and allow game instinct to flow. Where the will rules. Or not, in the case of players and teams that always seem to lose, at any level.

Turn momentum, turn the play and the worm turns to smile at you. Buck Showalter likes to say "the little white rat will find you" — meaning the ball will find your weaknesses. The game enforces its demands, always. If your shortstop's throwing shoulder is barking, he'll get that crucial grounder in the hole; if your third baseman has just taken a bad hop in the lip, the next one will come harder and hug the ground.

Quick infield outs that shut off incipient rallies are where the game really shines, for my money. That's where I feel most fully in it — there and rounding second, legging for third, looking for a wave.

The Gamer

From 1994 through '96 I played for the Kenyon College Lords, an NCAA Division III college baseball team in central Ohio. I was a full-time student at Kenyon, completing an undergrad degree twenty years late, and going through those first fall practices and scrimmages with new teammates 20-plus years my junior. Until the alumni game in early October, we were a mix of distracted strangers trying to jell into something resembling a baseball team. But that morning, the game changed us and gave us all a common ancestor.

The annual alumni game was an easy, breezy Saturday occasion where some alums would show up, we'd toss the ball around and listen to their stories, then play loose pickup innings on Kenyon's McCloskey Field. It was a break in the boot-camp routine of fall tryouts and workouts, with easier boundaries — the game played for sheer fun.

Our coach had received letters from an older alum, a fellow who'd graduated from Kenyon in 1949. Warren G. Moore, then 72 years young, was playing for the Fullerton Blues over–55 slow-pitch softball team out of California, traveling with them through the States, Europe, South America and New Zealand. He'd lost his wife a few years back, and had filled the intervening summers playing the ballgame he'd learned as a boy, in the company of other boys, exploring the edges of the game's play post–70.

Warren jetted in from California for this alumni game, showing up at practice on Friday afternoon decked out in his worn softball shorts and stretched kneesox, tossing the ball around and spitting out glorious bits of stories with a smirk. He won an attentive audience just by showing up, then delivered on the promise by showing us he could still throw, catch and twirl a bat.

Early the next morning he was there again, twitching to play. The day was nickel-gray and the air gentle, comfortably cool. We chose up sides and began an easy game. Warren led off the top of the first with a flair, choking up on his bat and singling through a drawn-in infield. He took a short lead at first base, hunched with his hands on his wrinkled knees, sox drawn up high. After a couple of flyball outs the shortstop gloved a grounder, and Warren gamboled toward second, where he was forced at the bag for the third out.

He chirped into the dugout for his glove, then back out to second base. And there, before the first pitch in the bottom of the first inning, he fell.

We watched him stagger, and sprinted out of the dugout as he collapsed. He sprawled on his back, puking and gagging, gasping for breath. We knelt over him, gasping ourselves. I cleared his throat and wiped puke from his stubbled chin to give him CPR, breathing puffs into his lungs then crawling over to his side to give him chest compressions, alternating these moves and trying to keep calm. My teammates clustered above us, pale in the face, bending over and urging him on. Suddenly rooted hard in our own lives, we tried to cheer him back up, back into the game.

A big Chevy roared across the outfield and the college's head trainer scrambled out to give me a hand, but he knew what he was seeing as soon as he got close. By the time the ambulance arrived Warren was gone. Right there, at second base, he gave it up.

The next morning Tracy Schermer, the college doctor, spent an hour with us sitting in a circle in the Great Hall, trying to reconcile what we'd witnessed — for most of these young players, a first close look at death. We settled upon a heartfelt sentiment, as easy and as hard as the game itself: Warren died doing what he loved best. He actually died playing. How else, the good doctor asked, would he have chosen to go, if choice were possible? It was most fitting for Warren to give it up right there at second base, surrounded by teammates generations along. His last at-bat was a hit. He died at his position.

It seemed like cold comfort at first, but it's held up like the proverbial one-run lead. Comes a time.

5

REALLY BUSH

So-Called Lords

The chance to finally play some college ball put a shine on my arrival in Ohio in late August of 1994. I landed feet-first into this wonderful tiny town and ancient stone campus (at least, ancient by American measure), feeling renewed by the old-growth trees and pebbled walkways, by all the bright human lights.

The first two students I met were throwing a baseball in front of their dorm as I rode by on my bike. I circled back. Pulling up at the curb, I introduced myself and announced to their amusement that I'd be trying out for the baseball team. Rhythm and Druba, two pitchers on the ball team, roommates and blood brothers, stopped tossing the ball to stand and gape. Their wonder, while seeming a bit strange to me then, makes all the sense in the world now. Kenyon is a homogenous sort of place, certainly in terms of the age of its students. A private four-year undergraduate liberal arts college with an enrollment of 1,500 and annual tuition approaching thirty grand, Kenyon is a privileged place to study, boasting a strong English department as well as other academic strengths. It's a school committed to teaching in the fullest sense it can imagine, a profoundly conservative academy of learning and ritual, striving to be that and more. Many of its faculty studied here as undergrads and managed to find their way back to stay. The students come from private prep and public schools, with a heavy tilt toward affluence and family tradition at Kenyon. A lot of students

53

come from Ohio and surrounding states, but others come from all over the U.S. and a few from abroad. The Kenyon swimmers are the powerhouse athletic team — both men's and women's teams are perennial NCAA Division III national champs. Kenyon and the village of Gambier fulfill the ideal of the academic hilltop, with a serious study regimen and students who pride themselves on working and playing hard.

Rhythm and Druba became my very fast friends, and did what they could to overcome the strangeness of age and deal with me as a peer. We had some good times, crawling through Kenyon's nightlife of frat parties and ritualized drinking games. They introduced me around in a collegial sort of way, and while I had not the time nor energy to partake fully, I did get a useful taste of it through their good graces. Kenyon kids were generally welcoming, though some never seemed to overcome suspicions of me. I tried to put them at ease, but spent much more time working and studying than trying to ingratiate myself. I hesitated to intrude, and on the few occasions I did mix I found some real openness and a lot of sophistry that peeled away quickly to reveal a lack of real experience and a multitude of time spent in front of television sets. They were kids, after all, though it was easy at times to forget that.

Out of this early welter of new faces and patterns came the long-awaited baseball tryouts. After the second day on the field, when I realized that I'd actually make this team, ankle notwithstanding — there was no not-making this team — I felt a tinge of competitive letdown mixed with optimism. Kenyon has a long history of intercollegiate baseball, going back to nineteenth-century Ivy League railroad games. The Lords have brought home losing records for over a hundred years with rare, wild winning streaks in between. Current prospects were consistent with this tradition, recent teams struggling to post double-digit wins in each forty-game season.

But all of that aside, the prospect of year-round ball with a college team was a dream spectacle, at this point in my life. I'd always loved practicing and playing games. The workingman leagues in which I'd played for the last ten years — full of cops and teachers and teamsters — had few midweek practices, sparsely attended. The games were all. Rosie and I would sometimes work out at Eisenhower Park, just the two of us — with flyballs for him, grounders for me, and hard BP for both with

Lords a-looking 1995.

a bucket of balls, galloping out to pasture to gather them up after each turn at-bat. I could do that every day and be a peaceful man.

In those first practice-and-scrimmage weeks at Kenyon I wore an air-cast and rubber cleats to protect the tender ankle. My lateral range at second was pathetic — I just couldn't move well from side to side. But the arm was good after a full season with the Bombers, I could sprint in a straight line, and I hit the ball a bit. We beat a cross-town rival college, the Naz — a good team — in a scrimmage, and my right-alley double got us back in that game. That's my clearest and dearest recollection from McCloskey Field.

The regular Kenyon second baseman was a third-year guy — a good, quick, compact player, skilled and drilled, the best fundamental infielder on the team. And he could stroke the ball. So I worked behind him, and as the ankle healed I tried to show capability somewhere it was needed, like third. But the coach had me depth-charted as a pinch hitter, seeing me as his Kirk Gibson, limp and all. But I was not that.

A couple of failed pinch-hit at-bats and he called it off, benching me for the season. I spent my time trying to keep the spirit up and the body ready, doing sprints, catching in the bullpen, backing up starters during infield drills, feeling about as happy as a wet cat.

I had one full-game start that season, playing second in another game at the Naz. Walked and scored three times, then hit one to the warning track in left. Played steady at second, and felt fluid in the field despite the lack of playing time. Nothing spectacular, but a start. String some of those together and you see what you got. But the innings didn't come. The same nine lost game after game. The bottom line was inexperience speaking for itself over and over, the same losing lineup, two seasons long. Truly, seasons in hell.

Wish fulfillment and denial are powerful contraries, and those two seasons— with an occasional pinch-hit at bat or cold inning in the field — were too fragmented to produce anything, or for it even to matter. It was the game constricted to a losing proposition, with occasional flashes of solid team play that were too precious to believe in.

Finally, it was a class thing. The workingmen who'd been my teams for the past decade were bred differently from these Lords, and knew what class was, and how to work and win with it. Baseball has blue-collar blood and sensibility at the best amateur levels; the Lords were just too refined in an odd way to play it well. The few working-class kids on the team — good-enough ballplayers— were not-so-subtly segregated. And the coaches, for all their self-supposed knowledge of the game, couldn't resolve the difference between a player's ability to do one thing well, and a team's inability to really play the whole game. Their depth charts drew a curtain over the holes in their players' souls, big enough for a rash of simple grounders to just dribble on through, or an easy flyball to drop in with a game on the line. The game, finally, does not take place in a coach's brain, or a player's pipe dreams; it takes the whole body and good instincts, the ability to swallow injury and fear and use them as fuel for finding ways to win. Absent that, fantasy gives way to the reality of the empty belly and the losing column. No matter how you decorate it — overseed the field, paint the dugouts, outfit the team with snazzy uniforms— when the game is played without soul, it gives back nothing but loss.

But all such bitterness, once indulged, is soon let go. You cannot play the next game while holding on to the last one. And you don't get any do-overs—you just get the chance to try again. For that, I'm more than grateful. Losing with the Lords would be a wasted way to end the effort.

Happily, their more recent story gets better. The 1998 Lords broke Kenyon's hundred-year record for most wins in a season (the new coach wisely downplaying that pathetic legacy as they approached the stupendous glory of 13 victories). With a lot of heart, they won a batch of early games in Florida, sagged a bit when they returned to Ohio's post-winter, then recovered focus and finished the season 16–17. True to form, the Kenyon curse brought rainouts for their final doubleheader against sad-sack Oberlin, washing out the prospect — the useful goal — of finishing over .500. But all season long, a very game young lefty named Mitch Swaggert showed everyone what heart and focus can accomplish — when he wasn't baffling hitters with a devastating changeup from the mound, he was hauling down liners in the outfield gaps like young Willie Mays. And he's here for two more seasons. Chris Schwoy, a working-class kid from Baltimore, contributed spectacular play at third and a commanding single-minded focus in the dugout.

So there's hope for these guys—all reaching for workingman baseball soul and drive, game for glory. It's there for the taking. And we root hard for all the heart they show, lifting each other up.

Sunday Angels

We began as Angels and devolved into Warthogs. Such is the amateur game in all its symbolic and animalistic glory. We entered the food chain of the Columbus, Ohio, MSBL in the summer of 1996 as the Columbus Angels, playing in B-Division. A year later the team split into the revolving-door Warthogs and the upstart DiamondBacks, and in that schism lies an ironic twist and some lessons in collective heart.

I found the Angels via manager Mark Davis* after calling the Columbus MSBL looking for a team. Mark came down to a Lords game at Otterbein College in Westerville on a sunny afternoon in early May to see me play. I was benched, as usual, so I asked the coach if I could throw down in the bullpen. He lent me a catcher, and I threw to Mac

Daddy for ten minutes while Mark watched from the other side of the fence. Later, behind the dugout, I tried on an Angels jersey and the deal was done.

We campaigned hard that summer, some new blood transfused into a team that had won only three games the previous year. We captured the B-Division title on the basis of solid pitching from the crafty righty Bill Heward and the lefty finesse of Nate Hamilton. Our closer, Alan Foe, threw smoke, leading the League in ERA at 0.65. The defense performed well, with gritty infield play and the occasional lapses backed up with solid recoveries— almost as if we were putting guys on base and daring them to try to score, managing to cut them down more often than not. Basically, we hit enough to win, though we seldom blew anyone out. For that level of play, we were solid enough to outlast most teams and capitalize on their mistakes while minimizing our own, though our baserunning was like a Chinese fire drill at times.

We played most of our games at McCoy Field, south of downtown Columbus, hard by I-71 and the trailer parks. McCoy was a mess of a field, with a lumpy infield, an overgrown outfield and a pitcher's mound that looked strafed and bombed. Its epitome was its lights, which would sometimes cut off in the middle of a late-night inning, engendering a sense of coitus interruptus. We'd break into the control panel and flip the lights back on, but it took them 20 minutes to heat up. We'd sometimes be there past midnight on a Thursday, trying to get 9 innings in. After a win, in the grassy darkness among the cars, Heward would light his cigar and coolers of Cokes and beers would appear from his trunk. We'd relive the victory or throw an impromptu wake for a loss. The Angels finished 16–7 on the regular season, with Bill's lucky victory cigars burning down to fine ash.

The righty/left combo of Heward and Hamilton got it done, both showing sure mound presence all the way. Bill threw hard righty cutters and low fastballs, while Nate slid lefty swerves at the corners. He always had a slower curveball on the spot where he needed it. They pitched us through 6 or 7 innings each time, sometimes solo, sometimes in tandem. Having Alan at shortstop for those innings gave us a solid glove there, with me at second, Jerry Miller or Scott Greisheimer at third, and a succession of steel-gloved first basemen. Alan was a force as a closer, throwing hard low heat and a big sweeping curveball that dive-bombed out of nowhere. I'd slide over to short when Alan took the mound — his strikeouts made me a solid late-inning choice there.

We went to the semifinal round of the League Playoffs before taking a pounding from the powerful BlackRocks, who had taken the A-Division title. The Warthogs finished just behind us in the B-Division, and over the next winter our coach (the cagey Davis) conspired with theirs (the cheeky Doug Smith*) to combine teams and move up to the A-Division, where the BlackRocks ruled. They figured that the best of ours and the best of theirs would be good enough to compete solidly in A. Mark showed restrained optimism, while Doug was convinced we'd win it all, from the get-go.

That spring, Mark got the word out early that no one was being handed a starting role in advance, and that everyone would be trying out for what was essentially a new team, with all positions open to the best player. He was combing central Ohio for good over–30 ballplayers, and would go with the best. I liked that, feeling the competitive fires glow even then, in the dead of the Ohio winter. Others were not so thrilled, and by the time we were three weeks into the winter indoor drills, a bunch had already dropped off the roster, seeing limited playing time ahead under Mark's new plan.

MSBL amateurs are the ultimate free agents; we can jump teams at will in the off season, while during the season we do so only with both coaches' and the league's permission. It's just enough restriction to keep teams intact during each campaign and avoid roster-shuffling for playoffs. Generally, it allows guys to find their best level, and to find teams with which they can live happily and get the playing time they want.

The Baseball Academy was our winter home, up in an industrial park in Dublin, north of Columbus. Our indoor Warthog workouts settled into a groove with a regular set of 9 and a revolving door of new faces, guys scouted out by Mark, mostly by reputation. A couple stuck, living up to advance billing. Most didn't. The regulars were looking solid but not real deep, beyond a single set of starters. We'd lost some undervalued walkaways to the upstart DiamondBacks, where they were welcome and guaranteed playing time.

The pitchers threw off plastic mounds to the catchers, while the rest of us hit live BP on the other side of the room. We'd finish each week with grounders off the carpet, doing two and out. Mark got real good at hitting the seam that runs the length of the astroturf, making the grounders move like those we were used to seeing at McCoy Field, where every ground ball is an object lesson in bad hops.

Early on, things were looking good on the pitching front: Mark had three new lefties, one of whom had thrown at AAA for Cleveland. And two righties, both of whom threw fairly hard with some stuff. I caught them all during those indoor weeks, and when Mark asked for reports I'd give them straight up, telling him where I was impressed with these guys, and which of their pitches seemed stronger or weaker. A staff was shaping up, and he was already putting together rotations and bullpens and campaign strategies in his spreadsheet.

Bill Heward was staying the course, in spite of the competition from the younger stallions. Bill's 48 now, a lanky bulldog righty who slings a mix of good low stuff, with fire in his belly on every pitch. He's a professor at Ohio State, and brings a hard-nosed, educated class to the dugout and a set jaw to the mound.

The war of attrition began with our outdoor workouts in May. PT, our AAA lefty, dropped out after feeling an old shoulder injury flare up. He asked Mark to keep him on the roster, and said he'd try again when the weather got warmer, and Mark hopefully consented, since PT would be a Number 1 horse on any staff in this league. Then Nate bailed, seeing his innings numbered by the long line of hard throwers ahead of him in this pack. He went over to the DiamondBacks with Mark's blessing, and with all good wishes from the rest of us. In truth, we hated to lose him. As fate would have it, Nate and the DiamondBacks would refuse to play like rejects, going far deeper than us in that next September's playoffs.

And therein lies the twist. Mark was so intent on building a winner with the Warthogs that he failed to value the Angels he already had. His newfound studs were not, finally, the ones who'd show up on hot Sundays in July and August. What was left after the DiamondBack defections was often simply 9, and even when it was the best 9, it wasn't always enough. We dropped some games by virtue of thin ranks, injury and irony — players playing out of position, trying to do what they didn't do best.

Meanwhile, the DiamondBacks beat everyone in their path, winning the B-Division easily. In the first three rounds of playoffs they shocked the league by blowing past teams that had been solid A-Division contenders during the regular season. They thrashed their way to the finals, a single championship game with the BlackRocks. The Rocks rocked early in that penultimate game, and the Backs rocked back. Tied at the end of nine, they battled on into the twelfth, when the Rocks wrested the game away with a single run, 13–12.

The DiamondBacks, then and there, were winners of a longer victory over low expectations, besting the campaign for their dignity with sheer will to win and an abiding habit of getting the game right. We Warthogs squandered our chances; the Backs grabbed theirs and held on for the whole ride. You've got to hand it to them — they had themselves a sweet season, one that'll glow the whole winter.

Keith Osik

I was driving south on Ohio Route 13 from Richland County toward my home in Knox County on a mid–April evening. The sky was showing some nice color, with high pink-and-purple clouds.

The Cincinnati Reds were on the radio from Pittsburgh via WTVS-AM in Columbus, trying to reverse an early slide, a stack of losses on their first road trip of the season. Last night they had dropped another close one, despite a throwing error in the ninth by the young Pirate catcher, Jason Kendall, which brought a run in and put the tying one on third. Listening to that game, I had wondered whether the other young Pirate catcher, Keith Osik, would get the next start, and now, sure enough, up he steps to the plate, with the Reds color announcer mangling his name ("Ahh-sik") and the stadium PA voice getting it right in the radio background ("Ohh-sik"). That booming, hollow radio echo sounds like a stadium runway tunnel, if you're of a mind to hear it that way. And I was. "Osik's looking for his first hit of the young season," drones the color man. "Walked his first time up. Bottom of the fourth, two out. Dave Burba on the mound for Cincinnati, and throwing well tonight. The Reds hold a 3-to-1 lead. And heeere's the pitch from Burba: (Crack!) A hard single into left, and Osik rounds first..."

The soft Ohio hills were making the radio wobble and fade, and I was watching Keith in memory from a few years back. His step-brother

Eric played with the Cardinals—a brick shithouse of a catcher and a heavy hitter. We had six guys from the Shoreham–Wading River High School team — the soon-to-be New York State Champs—on our snowflake team that fall. But we didn't have Keith. He played for Runyon's Yankees, the best amateur team in New York City. Runyons beat up every New York area opponent they faced, and traveled to regionals to beat the big boys from elsewhere. Keith caught, pitched, played short, all of it better than anybody we knew. He went on to LSU a year later, played every position one game, played in the College World Series, and was drafted by the Pirates. In the professional minor leagues he was an impact player, hitting .300 plus at every level until his first year in AAA, where he hit .230 or so. But the next season at Buffalo he took his stroke back over .300, and he was in the bigs in the fall, then back for good the next season, this one past. In 200 plus at-bats he hit .293, and it looks like he's there to stay, getting some innings behind the young star Jason Kendall. He filled in at third for the Pirates and even get some mound time in a blowout — a complete ballplayer, even as he rides the big bench.

More interesting to me than his major league exploits is his history as a glorious semipro player. He had this long and looping swing, which was also incredibly quick. He clubbed home runs to all fields against amateur pitching. And he played everywhere, wherever they needed a strong gun. In the old days, he'd have been a hot commodity for company teams and union teams and town teams. Runyon's was a force to be reckoned with in big-town Bushville, and Keith was the kingpin.

My last game with Keith came six years ago—poetically enough, on Doubleday Field in Cooperstown. Doubleday is a tiny, historic old ballfield packed to the rafters with ghosts— Babe Ruth played there, and Ty Cobb, and all the big-league greats. It has these tiny set-in dugouts that barely hold nine. Insufferably, our weekend series against Runyons was washed out on Friday and Saturday by a bitter upstate rain. The caretaker at Doubleday was being protective of his soggy shrine and wouldn't let us near the field in the rain, where we'd have happily played in sleet and snow. But on Sunday morning the skies finally cleared, and we got in a single game. Trotting onto that infield filled us with a blunt sense of kinship with the great players of the ages, a taste of present history right there in the brick dust. Joyfully haunted. Keith pitched the first three innings against us, and I was proud to bounce a hard grounder right at the second baseman for an out. We held them for three innings, and then a seam broke and they started pounding us deep. Keith hit a homer completely out of the park in left to cap that rally.

In the fourth inning, now catching, he picked me off second, me with a modest lead after a modest walk and a wild pitch. From his knees, he cut me down like a whipsaw, his throw to the creeping short-stop too quick to even mention. He took me to school, and gave me a quick glimpse of another level of play.

Now, the road banks over the tracks and down into Mount Vernon as the twilight fades. The Pirate home inning dies with Keith on second, and local radio commercials take over. I think about being in the game, and feel as absolutely there as Keith is now.

Stink

You often hear baseball fans passing judgment on some struggling player by saying "that guy stinks" or some such. It's a common statement by fans regarding major league players, but it's not a reasoned one. In fact, it's so far off that it's laughable. But you hear it all the time.

The fallacy of the remark lies in the fact that the player in question may be having a dry week or a bad month, but he's in the bigs. He's managed to rise through the ranks all the way to the top of his profession — and it's what we call baseball. He may be overpaid now, but he hasn't always been. There's a pack of hungry guys in the high minors just itching to get their shot at his job. No matter what his performance in a given month or season, no way does he stink. His skills are quite impressive. This would become most clear if you faced him in a local ballgame.

Many, many very, very good ones never made it to the bigs. And many, many of them didn't stink either. We've watched them and faced them in local ballgames for generations now, and found this to be so. Lives have stories, and you can believe them.

Really Bush

You hear this, too, from time to time — uttered as an expletive (often accompanied by others) — one player accusing another of acting in a manner that's second-rate. The offending opponent may have just slid in awkwardly with spikes high, or thrown his bat at the pitcher, or tried the hidden-ball trick in an obvious and unsuccessful way. The accuser's lips curl up and he spits out: "That's really BUSH!" It's an insult meant to imply that the offending player has acted in a manner that's beneath contempt, and in so doing has sullied the game itself. Players have come to blows over this particular accusation, whereas comments about your sister often pass without violence.

I've always been amazed by amateurs accusing other amateurs of being "bush." The origins of the usage lie in the expression "bush league," a perjorative term referring to the professional minor leagues from roughly 1905 onward. It would be most appropriately used by a major leaguer to accuse another major leaguer of belonging in the minors. But you hear it all the time in the amateur leagues, and it begs the question: if he's bush, what the hell are you? We're all bush! Actually, if you wanna get technical about it, we're less than bush. We're not being paid to play this game (as real minor leaguers are); therefore, being bush would constitute a promotion for us (and a wet dream).

I love it. It's a clear example of how amateurs so love the game, they come to see themselves as engaging it at a higher level, encasing themselves in an aura of professionalism to locate game respect. By the same token, when amateurs act really bush, they do sully the game. When they bitch and whine and throw things around, they act like spoiled kids who don't belong on the playing field. Interestingly, when big leaguers do likewise, they're truly bush, no matter how much they're paid, and no matter what kinds of numbers they put up. Give me an amateur with respect for the game's decorum over a big league tantrum any time.

Once in Arizona, at a national tournament, I watched a truly amateur player take a lead off second and frantically try to flash signs at the batter. His team was three runs down in the ninth inning, with one out; this player at second represented a meaningless run, unless others could follow. So, by the book, the runner should take a conservative lead, not take any chances at being thrown out on the bases or picked off, and hope the batter can get himself on base, and thereby prolong the inning. Well, this guy at second is out there waving his arms, and the batter swings at the first pitch and tops a weak grounder toward first. The first baseman picks up the ball and steps on the bag for the second out, letting the meaningless runner advance to third. It's called trading bases for outs; if that runner scores, the team in the field still has a two-run lead and needs only one more out. Good teams trade bases and runs for outs, as such opportunities present themselves, to close out a win.

But lo and behold — the meaningless runner doesn't stop at third. He rounds the bag, head down, and chugs for home with the first baseman standing at first, holding the ball. About the worst baserunning decision I'd ever seen. The results were predictable: an easy toss from the first baseman to the catcher, who waits for the runner and easily tags him out. Game over.

But lo and behold: the knuckleheaded runner jumps up and starts shouting at the previous batter, who'd just grounded out to first: "What are you doing?! Didn't you see me give you the take sign?!! I was going to steal third!! YOU JUST COST US THE GAME!!!"

Really bush.

Snowflake

An umpire stands waiting for the sides to change between innings, waving his arms and flexing his legs like one very cold monkey. He's got his long underwear on under his regulation gray polyester slacks, and gloves and a scarf beneath his blue blazer. None of these layers are very effective against the cold wind blowing in from right-center, over the soft hills of the town dump. That wind is coursing down from the north off the Long Island Sound, spilling over the rocky north shore and picking up dump gas on its way to these Flynn Park diamonds in Smithtown. The landfill smell is sickly-sour as opposed to sickly-sweet, with undertones of natural sugars and syrupy goo being crushed out of untold tons of household garbage 200 yards away. My pals who worked on garbage trucks called it hopper juice. Beneath the dump hills somewhere is a fetid lake of it, and its essence is a constant companion for player, fan and umpire alike.

During summer day games the dump stink permeates the clay and you end up tasting it all the way home. On warm summer nights it forms a fog that rolls down off the sand-covered hills to hang in the lights of Flynn's three softball diamonds and one blessed baseball field. And on cold autumn nights like this one it bites with the wind, finding its way to your skin through every seam. It's not so bad if you're playing; layers of sweat and adrenaline and exertion keep you sort of warm. But umpires have it tough; it's much harder to keep warm when you're standing around. Every gust of wind feels colder than the last, and the deep chill seems to slow the game down.

Flynn Field is a tough one even on the best of nights. The four fields are arranged in a larger diamond, with all the home plates gathered at the quadrant's center. The ring of surrounding outfield lights, low and bright, make it most challenging to play here. Your entire view — the whole panorama — is filled with a bright hi-beam haze. Low liners disappear into that humming light-bank, causing outfielders to step and then falter, suddenly unsure of just where the ball is going; in a heavy dump fog, flyballs just vanish completely up into the bright night haze, leaving the outfielders running in panicked circles, covering their heads.

Animals sometimes find their way out onto the playing field, so the outfielders are further distracted by dump foxes, rabbits and scampering rats. Beyond the outfield fence is a frightening backdrop — the putrid smell adding a wretched dimension to the black outlines of the hills, the angular earth-moving equipment, and clouds scudding through a menacing sky.

On one particularly fragrant evening a drunken seagull came coasting in low over the outfielders' heads toward the infield, trained on the backstop as a homing beacon. This large white bird tilted in his slow glide, seeming unable to focus, and sailed directly — slowly and deliberately — right into the backstop fence, with the batter, catcher and umpire all diving out of its flight path. Crashing into the chain link and falling in a heap behind home plate, it slowly arose, shook itself off, took a few awkward hops and was airborne again, motoring now at low altitude back toward whence it had come, homing in on the dump hills. The game paused until the gull barely cleared the outfield fence, and as the outfielders watched it chug off into the smelly darkness they smirked at each other and shuddered to themselves.

Two days later, on my morning commute to work along the Northern State Parkway in slow traffic, I came upon that seagull — I think it was him — as he snarled traffic for ten minutes by flying at headlight level with the westbound cars, slowly gliding along three feet off the macadam with its eyes glued on the double yellow lines. This bird clearly had a substance abuse problem, and the substance in question was something it supped on at the dump. Or maybe, I thought as I drove slowly behind him, maybe just too many flights through that gas.

♦

The snowflake season brings all such elements together for a mercifully-brief six weeks in October and November. Teams play one night game and a Sunday doubleheader each week, getting in another twenty games or so after the summer season and playoffs are done. Under the cold conditions, the game's edges harden a bit; play becomes just a bit more brittle; pitchers blow into their hands to keep some sort of feel and grip on the ball. Hitters have to contend with what we called the handful of bees: if you fail to hit the ball squarely, worse yet get jammed off the bat handle, you get this intense stinging sensation as bat hits ball, and for several long minutes afterward. With your hands cold to begin with, the pain really burns. Pitchers who can keep their grip and control in the cold will bust batters inside and hope to lend them some of that self-same pain to occupy the better part of their attention. But fielders tend not to get the best jump on the ball when they're doing jumping jacks to keep warm, so the disadvantages even out. Everyone has to deal with the cold and stiffness, and the occasional random snowflake does little to cheer the scene.

Aside from the drunken seagull, my fondest Snowflake memory is of Rob Marto, a 230-pound bearcub of a Stony Brook Cardinal just learning to chew tobacco. He didn't quite have his spit mechanics down, so he'd just slobber brown chaw juice all over the dugout whenever he opened his mouth. Everything was stained brown: the baseballs, the helmets, even our mitts. We learned to hang precious things on the fence rather than drop them on the dugout floor, because Marto's hopper juice would fly anywhere at any time without warning.

Snowflake at Flynn was the game at its furthest wretched reach, played with a blind, shivering devotion long past its proper season.

That umpire doing St. Vitus' Dance between innings shed real tears on some of those nights, crying and snarling at the players, the game, and the ball itself to hurry up and get this thing over with. We'd see the tears on his face and we'd smirk vengefully; pause to tie a shoe in the batter's box; scratch with deliberation and a grim smile around the infield. Our purposes were flavored by the dump gas and colored by Marto's fiery brown slurry, a dark palette of little horrors under cold, bright lights, late on a lunar baseball night.

Eye

I struggled with the bat this past season with the Warthogs. I was streaky, hitting well for a couple games then sliding into a material funk that would last for weeks. I resisted the urge to tinker with mechanics and just went up looking for pitches to hit, but I was just off — getting decent swings but not making great contact, popping up and pounding balls hard into the ground. It seemed, at times, like I wasn't seeing the ball. The eyes do fade in your forties.

Don Mattingly advocated specific training for good baseball eyes. He endorsed an eye-exercise device that I used once or twice — a large board that you face closely, with dozens of small lights that come on, one at a time, in a random pattern across a tight grid. You stare straight ahead and use your peripheral vision to spot each light as it blinks on, trying to touch it before it blinks off. You can adjust the levels of speed and randomness. Donnie Baseball supposedly used this device to keep his hitting eye strong.

Peripheral vision is much more acute at seeing motion than our straight-on vision. I sometimes wonder if Mattingly actually avoided staring at the ball, looking off a bit to allow his peripheral vision to do the work. I've tried it in the cage — it's a scary tactic with hardballs hurtling at you. But then, Mattingly played beyond scary.

The truth is, undisciplined vision can distract a ballplayer, young or old. You see batters looking around the diamond instead of staring through the pitcher to watch the ball he hides behind him. In the field, you see players literally look ahead to the throw before they make the catch, and thus not make the catch. It takes quiet, steady eyes to play the game best. Good outfielders learn to run in a way that allows them a steady view of flyballs off to either side. Infielders tend to bounce more when they run, and sometimes lose flyballs in that visual hip-hop.

The best athletes in most sports take best advantage of clear and focused vision — literal vision, which is figurative. It's used by the best players to great advantage. But you don't hear much talk about it.

Heads and hands, the Gorillas used to say. It was one of our dugout mantras. We were young and winning, with quick feet and steady eyes. The head holds the eyes and the brain, which take the willing body through the dance. When you dive for a ball and see it into your glove, the eyes are fluid and ready to see the play through, and the rest follows.

6

HITTING THE WALL

Team

You watch your mates through a big play, moving yourself as the ball arcs through the infield, roping confidence through everyone like a shared lifeline. With fine execution in this practiced turn in the dance, an out is taken. The immediate payoff is this sense of invincibility — we can do this, these runners mean nothing. Erase them. Get us back in the dugout to grab some bats, just two more outs.

Time breaks as the confident swell circulates around the horn, with looks and postures flexing. The field settles as the next one steps to the plate, looking around for a hole. We rock side to side to gauge those gaps ourselves, three steps and a dive toward the middle, or hard in for a slow roller. You rock, anticipating. The pitcher rocks.

His pitch brings a cracking swing and a line shot to the hole the other way, first base side. You're leaning there then winging it, two long steps and a dive right out, mitt hand reaching for the thigh-high liner. Seeing it, squeezing it in, it all falls together instantly. From the dirt, you sprawl to your knees and sidearm the ball low to first. The runner's doubled up on a short-hop catch, by a half-arm's length, and you get the call.

Trot for the dugout like you're hopping through surf, the glory washing up and all around, enough for everyone but them in the other dugout. You intersect your first baseman, find his eyes and chatter, "Pick it, Wilson." You hand off the glory and in so doing, find a team. Giving to get. Set for the moment.

Oyster Bay Bombers 1994.

Blue

Quality of umpiring is always an issue in amateur leagues. You hope for it to match the level of play, or at least come close, but you don't always get that. Mediocre umpires are tolerable at the lowest levels of play — the skills of Little Leaguers and young scholastic teams generally make the close calls less crucial to a game's outcome, because young players and teams struggle to make even routine plays consistently. As playing skill rises, close calls become more pivotal. The team that makes the routine and the extraordinary plays — and gets the calls — rules the day. But when a team makes big plays and the ump misses them — by not hustling to get into position to make the right call, or by an inability to judge breaking-ball strikes (common among amateur umps) — then the umpiring drags down the overall level of play and the game itself. When strong play doesn't get the calls it should, or gets them inconsistently, it becomes less consistent, more distracted, losing the sharp edge of winning focus. Momentum shifts from sheer game-presence to ump-blaming and -baiting, sending the flow in another direction entirely.

When an ump makes himself the cross-eyed issue in winning and losing (an at-bat, an inning, or a game) he tilts baseball further into the realm of imperfection that has always been its essence, its blessing and its curse. In such circumstance the mix of luck and skill that spells success in all parts of the game (and everywhere else) veers off into imperfect unfairness, and that decides the day. With umpiring as elsewhere, it's a matter of degree: the tilt can be momentary or repetitive, a minor ripple in good flow or a cascade of misdirections. Like misplaced punctuation, it can, scramble the. Meaning.

The only thing worse than inadvertant spotlight-grabbing by an ump is its intentional evil twin. I've seen instances from youth leagues to the bigs where an umpire decides he's going to put on a show and redirect the course of the game by the sheer force of his ego, snarling at fans and players who question his judgment (and perhaps, his ancestry). The situation engendered for both winners and losers by a misfiring, grandstanding umpire harkens back to professional baseball's farcical 19th-century days, when the game's integrity was no article of faith. A willfully bad ump can besmirch a game like corruption itself, leaving a serious stink behind to test the spirit of fan and foe alike.

♦

Then there's the other side of the story. It's the umpire's side — which most of us choose to disregard and disparage. But the game's imperfect truth arises from there. The umpire's view is central.

Umpires are athletes playing inside the game. They conduct it and punctuate it with outs and safe calls, fair and foul, strike and ball. The best umpiring is intrinsic; the game defines itself in flow and they confirm it, pitch by pitch and play by play. When umpires do the job without being noticed, and the play is the focus, you know they're good.

Umpires are all about rhythm and right. At the pro level, their skills can be as impressive as that of the ballplayers. Down here in the amateur trenches, the skill levels vary as widely as those of the athletes. And just as it does with players, the game's demands prove out the skills of an umpire, and his responses, in turn, define the game. Umps who fail to keep up and to establish control are begging for trouble. The bad ones fail to establish their own play-calling with any consistency, while also failing to communicate command to the dugouts. It gets ugly.

I got tossed for the first time in my life in a Warthogs game in Columbus a few summers past. The field ump's total lassitude was letting the game slip away. He was spacing out and making obviously bad calls, and both benches were barking at him. I had just peeled our first baseman off the ump after he blew a call at first, and I snarled at him as I pulled Mark away. With the next pitch that baserunner legs for second and we nail him at the top of his slide — great throw, easy swipe tag, no doubt about it. I hear the safe call and spin around with my mouth agape — and I'm gone in a speechless instant.

The irony of most baseball arguments is that the aggrieved player or coach is putting the cart before the horse: the horse won't pull, so he yells at the cart. It's a tempting diversion from the fact that the horses just can't seem to do it today. Umpires know this ruse and have scant respect for it.

Branch Rickey defined what it takes to be a good umpire in Shakespearean terms: "the authority of a sea captain, the discretion of a judge, the strength of an athlete, the eye of a hunter, the courage of a soldier, the patience of a saint and the stoicism to withstand the abuse of the grandstand, the tension of an extra-inning game, the invective of a player and the pain of a foul tip in the throat ... The players are faceless. The play's the thing."

As a player and as a coach, here's what's reasonable to ask of an amateur umpire: Along with knowing the rules completely, and knowing where he should be — how to locate himself for making the right calls — an umpire has to hustle mentally to stay at the level of play. He has to see the game for what it is, and stay right with it, knowing what to expect of it. Fact is, poor play often leads to poor play-calling; when players sag and shy away from the game, umps do likewise. Bad umpiring can strain a game into a wobble; but more often in the mud leagues, a wobbly game skews calls. What the umpire gives you, you earn. The burden lies with players and coaches to make the game brilliant, and with umps to know brilliance when they see it.

It's reasonable to demand of umpires that they stay with the game at its actual level of play. Best case, with both teams playing well, executing, making good throws, turning routine plays and rising to make fine ones, the umpire punctuates the positive accurately and cleanly. He hustles and keeps his focus, using his eyes as his first tools, just like the players. If he can't do all of that, he shouldn't be working that game.

♦

As this baseball season begins we're seeing a new mix of umpires in the bigs—actually, many of the same guys, but with a new union in place and 20-odd new members. Last fall the previous union head made the tactical miscalculation of encouraging his members to resign en masse to force early talks with the national office. His plan backfired when umpires broke ranks, some hurriedly withdrawing their resignations. For once, the national office played to its strength, accepting selected resignations and forcing a crisis in the union's leadership, which led to quorum of umpires abandoning that union and forming the new one. Major League Baseball set up a working agreement with the new union, abolishing ties to the now-defunct National and American League offices and pulling the umpires under central control. Not nearly a complete solution, it does seem to have weakened the choke-hold of union-protected umpires drunk with their own power and eager to brawl.

A more complete solution would create a merit system for umpires, extending from the independent professional leagues right up through the bigs. Umpires would be watched and rated, with the best moving up and the worst moving down year to year (like players, go figure). Pay grades would increase at each level, with the most money in the bigs, but a reasonable working salary at all professional levels. Pains would be taken to minimize political weight in the ratings, and to maintain a fair system promoting good work and rewarding the best with advancement and the worst with demotion. Umps scoring poorly year after year would be encouraged to leave the profession. It's a very tough job and not everyone can do it well.

Making umpires accountable for poor performance and rewarding them handsomely for good work makes all the sense in the world if you love the game. It aligns game-calling with the game itself, demanding athletics of body, mind and vision. Clear consequences for bad umpiring — blowing calls, not calling the game by the rules — and especially for bad umpire behavior, like pursuing players across the field to argue — would move the worst out and bring the best forward. Get this: in recent years certain big league umpires have been worse role models than certain players. A lack of consequence results in poor performance and attitudes to match.

At the most basic level, the game must be called by the rules outlined in the rulebook. That demands enforcement. It's not "my strike zone" it's THE strike zone. Like home plate, it's 17 inches wide — or, if you take the view that a strike means any part of the ball touching any part of the zone, that widens it by a mere couple inches on either side of the plate, for about 21 inches total. Not 36 inches, which is the way many big league umps have been calling it in recent seasons (and thus, the amateurs who take their cue from watching them). The strike zone's highest point is below the hitter's letters, not at the belt. Umpires need to give the high strike back to the pitchers, while taking away the inside/outside strikes that batters truly can't reach.

I think there should be a cap on the years of service allowed for field-umpiring Major League Baseball. After reaching the bigs and rating highly enough year after year to stay there, for perhaps 15 years, umpires should be promoted into an organization that manages the training, certifying, rating and managing of umpires. Evaluations should be conducted by these emeritus umps with input from coaches, players and baseball writers, as well as from fans in some limited way. Senior management should create umpire training for amateur leagues nationwide, sponsoring clinics to spread the gospel of good game-calling and to recruit the best local umps for professional work. Most importantly, the official scorer of each Major League game should be a senior umpire — one of the very best — rather than a local sportswriter. Hits and errors count; an umpiring eminence should obviously be making those calls. Such a system would make best use of hard-won umpiring wisdom.

Finally, umpires should be paid more. In the bigs, they should earn more than the players' minimum. They should have a clear career path that rewards hard work and strong, consistent performance, allowing them to earn a good living and show their best at successive levels. Ultimately, they should manage the conduct of the Major League game and exert strong influence on all that flows out from it — the quality of umpiring everywhere. With open ranks, an effective merit model and systematic leadership, there would be a better flow of younger umpires moving through the whole system, rather than a stagnant pool of elites at the top whose union protects them from their own nonperformance while keeping better umps stuck for life in Bushville.

At all levels, good umpires are the priests of the enterprise. There is hard-won and well-deserved pride among them, a deep understanding of the game and a sense of beleaguered purpose. They share a calling, and the catcalls are all part of it. Nose-to-nose with an angry strikeout victim, they hold the line and keep it a game.

Infield-In

It's an act of reduction within the game — a sudden shortening of the distance between you (infielder) and the batter.

A runner on third in a close game, where you need to keep that run from scoring at any cost — that's what sets it up. Usually a hand signal or a whistle from the dugout calls it, but an alert infield will creep in on its own, sometimes on a nod from the shortstop. Everyone edges in to the grass in front of the baselines from their normal distances somewhere ten or fifteen feet beyond them.

Dividing that crucial measure — the distance from fielder to batter — down to its shortest possibility tests infielders' quickness, where a hard-hit ball to either side will skip through but for a quick diving grab; or a ground shot right at you will drop you down to block it or else, eat you up. The angles are cut most severely — your triangle on the batted ball much more acute. Game sense likewise — keyed up on your literal toes, drawn closer into the action to give up the easy out for a play at the plate.

The stakes rise for the batter as well. He needs to get that run in. The infield is opening holes by coming closer, but all the batter sees is fielders, larger in his field of vision. If he's a good hitter he'll ignore them, swing down and hard, or try to drive the ball deep to score that run on a sacrifice fly. He's got more places to put hits, but for some batters, infield-in is more visual pressure than they like.

Around the infield, good players focus down as the stakes rise. Be most nimble now. Ready for the ball, any speed or angle or hop. Ready to charge a slow topper, or hang fire for a wicked linedrive. The dramatic possibilities multiply as adrenaline flows, pitch by pitch — too many sudden results to list. The irony is, in this situation, the hard-hit ball might not score the runner, while a dink swing may serve it to a spot where it would be an easy out for either of two players at normal position, but instead falls in, scores the runner and puts another on first.

Do or die. Infield-in is another brink, a verge beyond which things change one way or another. It's a gamble—trying to cut off one run, you give your opponent a better chance to score a bunch. But you also give your infield a shot at heroics, at crossing the boundary whole, and at holding on to this game at its quintessence.

Hanging Them Up

There comes a time. You may not see it coming—maybe you glide along thinking it'll never come. But it does. It sneaks up on you.

Time caught up with me after another long season of amateur ballgames, with 30 games in 30 weeks, another 30 workouts or practices—for 30 years or so—a good chunk of time spent on or around the diamond. You feel fatigue building over the course of progressive seasons—your legs deaden, your arm stiffens, you take longer to get loose before a game. Maybe your concentration slackens, or maybe it sharpens—everyone's different. Some guys get better as a season goes on, while others go slack. But we all get old, if we live that long.

The time does come, no question. I awoke one midnight and realized I couldn't move my right arm. It was like a part of me had died, filling with a hollow, drifting sort of pain. I tried to roll over on my side, but finally had to reach across with my left hand, grab the right arm, and yank it over the top—like a soldier rolling a fallen comrade over into a foxhole. That's when I knew the time was coming. Artillery was pounding nearer. Forget sleep.

Hanging them up is the pivotal point in a baseball life. Hold the ball. The game's over. No more lacing them up, no more shagging flies, no more running poles and infield drills. You relinquish that claim — not just upon youth (for all it's worth, good and bad) but basic capability. That loss is what aches. On a cool, clear evening not long ago, Angel Ted Covington chased a bounding ball at the leftfield fence of McCoy Field in downtown Columbus, Ohio. From shortstop, I watched the batter bolt out of the box, looking three as he rounded first. I ran out for the cutoff throw, caught it, spun and gunned that rabbit — third baseman Jerry Miller, his mouth still bleeding from a bad hop two innings earlier, gloving my throw and sweeping a perfect matador tag on the sliding hitter. Runner out, rally over, game soon won.

Right now, that throw would dribble, with the shoulder snapping like a loose guitar string. Comes a time, with heartache.

Trains

Like an echo across time, the sound of a train always brings a shine to my face at second base. It penetrates the shell of a game's occasion, defining rhythm in the soft cadence and specific clarity of a familiar glow. As in sex, where physical comfort and eagerness wrap the present tense of self and other in an immediate falling down, where music can take you partway out of the moment while fixing you there absolutely, the sound of a train brings to baseball a sweet prenatal signal.

Low, distant rumbles of boxcars-boxcars-boxcars punctuate a pitcher's fidgets on the mound and the swaying of the catcher's knees. There may be a breeze bringing the rumble way down low, rocking the field as the shortstop rocks on the balls of his feet. Or it might be a still August night with heavy air and a winsome whistle filtering in from way beyond an outfield fence. Turning for a moment, I see the outfielders stirring, peering in past me to the plate from their pools of night light. Darkness envelops this game's glow, glanced perhaps by the trainmen as they rollick slowly past with reciprocal longings.

I grew up with trains, as did the game. Day and night, our house shook with the passing of the Long Island Rail Road (the tracks barely a hundred feet from us, along Union Street). Our home sat almost exactly between the Babylon and Bay Shore stations, west and east, along the southern spur of the L-I-double-R. The railmen ran busy schedules for thousands of morning and evening rush-hour commuters, trundling empty trains back to railyards at night. Overnight guests in our home invariably had trouble sleeping, for the trains; we, on the other hand, would lie sleepless on nights when the trainmen walked off the job on strike. Somehow the absence of the trains made us restless.

Nineteenth-century college teams played weekend series with other schools in their region — now an easy flight or bus ride, then a voyage by rail across newly-imaginable distances. Back then, Kenyon played in a nascent collegiate league with Harvard, Yale, Penn, and other schools. Imagine the schoolboy thrill in riding to ballgames on a rocking train, sprawled on leather-trimmed benches and joking through the deepening evening, feeling brazen and big. Then curling up against the window with the moonlight seeping in, the traincar keeping track over sublime landscape. Far places becoming real and exalted, brought to the fore.

The big leagues also lived by rail in the early days. With all the teams clustered in the east — Pittsburgh, Cleveland, Chicago, St. Louis and Milwaukee holding the far western reaches for leagues centered in New York, Boston, Philadelphia and D.C. — major league schedules were driven by night-long train rides.

And with all the history of big league baseball yet to be realized, those nineteenth-century Kenyon players created a ghost legacy still in transit. On the ride home, tired and sore, flushed perhaps with games won or crestfallen with loss, rocking on rails, the players, still, come.

Now, the traveling game has been run from those rails. Other conveyances create the occasion. But the echo of a train from a ballfield brings all of time together and holds it for as long as the rumble and wail can hang in the air and resonate in clay. History stretches its legs in those moments, pauses and takes a deep breath, pulls on the brim of its cap, and leans in for the next pitch.

Hitting the Wall

So now, with snowflakes flying through the village lanes on a chill December wind, it comes down to this: another reduction of the game to its essentials. To practice. Going through the motions, quite literally, of pitching — playing precisely one-half of the overpass one-on-one game as an off-season workout routine. Solo, facing no hitter, a pitcher throws against a wall into a strike-zone box painted there (in this case, outlined by blue tape on a south wall inside Kenyon's

Wertheimer Fieldhouse). Under wintry skies the game comes in from the cold to work on base mechanics and to feel the sweat and glow.

All the familiar pregame rituals map to this reduction. Shed layers and stretch, for starters. Run a lap or two, then stretch some more: leaning into the wall for the hamstrings and calves; standing straight and holding each leg back to work the quads; deep bends, straight down, with legs tightly crossed to work the hamstrings and butt. Holding each set and feeling the burn work in. Down on the floor for butterflies, feet soles-together, working the groin and inner thighs. Then lay back with one knee up tight against your chest for the gluts and upper hams. All the while breathing slowly, deeply, deliberately, thoughtlessly — getting your whole self humming.

On your feet, you scan the expanse of the fieldhouse as you do a few final sideways bends and stretch your arm across your chest, using the other arm as a brace. Now shake it all out. The wall is calling.

Before you can throw hard you have to throw soft. Now more than ever, these muscle rehearsals are key for me. So the first few tosses against the wall are soft lobs, not aiming for the strike zone, happy to just hit the wall. With slow, exaggerated windups and rainbow throws it all starts to get in gear — the elbow snaps and shoulder muscles start slowly pumping up the jam.

The fieldhouse has a wooden mound stored off in a corner — a heavy woodframe construct sheathed in thick plywood, on a slant forward with a two-by-four pitching slab at the back. I drag it out and eyeball-align it with the blue strike zone, fifty-five feet away (throwing a little short this early in winter; longer later). Now, ready with a light sweat breaking, I go to work.

Usually, I do a set routine. Same way every time, only adjusting pitch count and mix depending on when I last threw and how my right arm feels. On a good day I'll throw ten more warmups from the mound, then start working counts with fastballs, changeups, and breaking balls—fifty to seventy pitches in all. When I'm sore I throw less and easier, no breaking balls. The entire routine gives me a taste while keeping mechanics intact, a very specific form of conditioning. By working fast I keep the sweat, getting a lot done in a little time. Sometimes I try new grips, release points and arm slots. But mostly I condition consistency and control, balance and presence there on that ramshackle mound. Feeling the game, reduced but reduced accurately. I work on a mindset that can bring the work off well and carry it over to summer afternoons and real fields.

Each pitch goes like this: Facing the zone straight-up with your right foot on the slab, right leg straight, left leg slightly back and bent a bit at the knee. You stand there with a slightly right-center balance point, the first balance point. Shoulders are tucked in consciously, arms up and in, parallel to your chest, with elbows near to touching; ball in hand in glove, with a light grip; the glove in front of the throat. From that stance you focus in visually on the zone and set the windup in motion.

Rock gently back onto the left leg and bring the arms up for an over-the-head windup. The hands peak just as lower-body balance begins to shift from the left leg to the right. As the weight transfers, your left leg comes up to a knee-cocked waist-level point as your arms come down to the belly. These two motions—leg coming up, arms coming down—wind the spring, which comes to a coil there at the chest, at the balance point. Poised there on your right leg, your body tucked in just a bit to keep your mass centered, you come to a flamingo position you should be able to hold for a full minute. It's worthwhile to drill just that—coming to that balance point and holding it, then stepping down and doing it again, same way every time.

Everything proceeds from that point, and if balance isn't there, everything proceeds badly. With balance, you can uncoil fluidly and forcefully toward home, bringing your pitching arm up and through its slot as your body drives off the slab, timing it to keep your weight back long enough (milliseconds matter) so as not to drag the arm behind. If you hit that timing mark, synchronizing your body mass and arm slot right on time, you can hurl the ball with accuracy and some stuff. You watch it hit the blue zone with a true thunk, then skitter right back to you. Bend over, glove it, then straighten up to do it again.

And again. Working counts, you ump your own pitches, judging whether or not each one hits your spot. The aim is not just to hit the zone, but to hit spots within it, purposefully. The lower-right corner is a tough one for most righty batters; upper-right might fool a lefty or back a righty away. Coming across to lower-left you might strike out a righty or get hammered by a lefty. Mostly, you try to move the ball around, avoiding the heart of the plate and working the corners, in and out, up and down, changing speeds. You set up one pitch with another: high fastball up and in on a righty (upper-right corner) then a curveball moving down and away (to lower-left). Your forkball might start in the zone, looking like a fastball, then dive straight down. When my arm feels right I can turn the ball over and get it to screw in on righties—a good out pitch if it jams their hands.

All of this follows with as much calm cool concentration and fluid grace as you can muster, pitch by pitch. You work the counts with honest discipline: balls are balls, strikes are strikes, and fat pitches are always hits. You can get into the flow of the game—just a trickle, but a steady one—by keeping tabs on each pitch, walking batters, pitching from a stretch as required, and letting the physical game take over—staying ahead of hitters, driving through the gutty out-pitch, and not giving in when you're behind.

When I get to sixty pitches or so I stop, do a quick inventory stretch there on the mound, then throw ten more hard strikes. Then I ease off, throw a few more easy lobs, and step off the mound feeling finished for now.

Everything works itself out against the wall on a cold snowy day, when all hope is lost to winter and the promise of spring (training) is only possible in a refuge such as this. Continuity with all other baseball moments is complete, and never complete. Hard to imagine not doing this. Outside, under a heavy coat, my shoulders glow.

7

BALLYARDS

Twilight

The time was ripe for me to discover the Twilight. Perched on the cusp of playing or no longer playing after my first summer off in many, with only the fieldhouse throwing to keep the slender thread connected, I'm surely in the twilight of my playing days. But twilight is gradual. It's a time of evening as the light lowers, a time in which visibility comes and goes. Having avoided catastrophic injury to this point, my good fortune is having this reckoning time to close in on the point when the game truly must walk off the field and call it a day.

Amidst all such off-season accounting I read an article about the Twilight League, 96 years young in southern Maine, and I traveled to the fair city of Portland to seek it out. Though I have only threads of it, the Twilight looms large in my imaginings of how to wrap it all up.

♦

The league's name comes from a pattern of playing weeknight games sans lights in southern Maine, at the far eastern edge of the Eastern Time Zone. Daylight fades early in down-east Maine. Dusk descends by 8:30 in high summer. As Yogi said of Yankee Stadium's old-time leftfield shadows, it gets late early out there.

Since 1903 the Twilight has been the mainstay of local baseball in Portland's environs. Pro minor league teams have come and gone — the Portland SeaDogs presently play as the Eastern League AA affiliate of

Minnetonka Millers in Neisville corn 1998.

the Florida Marlins—but the Twilight has been the constant, engaging scores of players and their families in a local baseball narrative flavored with New England's peculiar devotional reflexes and certainties. They played under the name Northern New England Semi-Pro League for a few years in the 1980s, then went back to the Twilight. Throughout the century they've played two single-game weeknights plus a Sunday doubleheader every week from June through August, 35–40 games in a season for each of six (now eight) teams. In their 96th year, they still play hardball on unlit fields in the evenings when they must, and under the lights when they can. Absent lights, they played seven-inning games for many years; now lighted fields allow for nine most of the time, passing through daylight's fade toward final frames under spare field light.

Teams come from two hours north of Portland and as far south as Portsmouth, New Hampshire. Players are scattered further, with some driving two hours just to get to a home game, sometimes another hour or so for a road game. For seasonal workmen, college kids on summer break and older guys with jobs and families, making hay while the sun shines, the Twilight League has been all about evening ballgames. Twice each week they went from work to the ballyard, direct, for a six p.m. start. They played Twilight ball for as long as light held, or a lead held, or a pitcher held a runner who could see him. Beyond a certain point came the gloaming—the dull glow of evening dusk, evening toward black, and no more game. Sundays brought daylight doubleheaders, but depending on the start time for the first game, the second might end in twilight all the same. All through the seasons, the last light of day worked its peculiar magic in making games fade out.

In time, more fields were rigged with lights—the first in Portland proper was Deering Oaks in 1980, then Hadlock Field saw lights go up. When they could get on those fields the Twilighters played in bright patchy pools downcast from lightpoles, taking games through to their natural end in unnatural illumination, with the shadows taking part in the action. Contention for lighted fields was always keen; all of the locals from age 13 and up vied to play under the lights on weeknights and even weekends. More often than not they made do without, and invariably twilight arrived to play its spoiler role.

Twilight defines the far edges of those unlit games, the late frames of a seven-inning contest. It's up to the umpire to call a game on account of darkness, and those that work the Twilight are generally willing to go as deep as possible, as far as the far edge of vision allows, until play becomes tentative and edgy, not to mention dangerous. As a player you begin seeing only half the ball, or less—it becomes a crescent, mostly shadow. As a bystander you wince at seeing a player fighting the sudden poor contrast and making false moves—stuttering steps, hesitating swings, the batter shaking his head in the box.

In deepening dusk, the game's form fades with waning definition. Twilight winners find ways to redouble their concentration and coax focus out of the receding daylight. They locate plain luck to become the beneficiaries of the fallen flyball and the shadowy grounder skipping past a blinking infielder with night rolling in and a game fading out.

Safe to say, there's been some justice and some injustice in all that. For 96 years the twilight's been an added dimension, a more whimsical, less predictable state of game. It can tilt either way, and has.

◆

The Twilight League began at Portland's Bayside Park in the first seasons of the 20th century, then moved to Deering Oaks in the 1940s. The league got a grant to install lights there in 1980, then Hadlock Field was lighted by the city in 1985. The Seadogs' home was named for Eddie Hadlock from Cornish, who played ball with Twilight president Bob Philbrick in Canada long ago then coached Portland High School for

25 years. Eddie was a great pitcher in his time, and a beloved coach. Thankfully his name remains on the city's best ballpark. With some agony and irony, the Twilight League can no longer play on Hadlock — the Seadogs have exclusive use. Eddie's great amateur name now graces the professional game while shutting out his own.

◆

Like any league, the Twilight has had its heydays and its flat water. It's in a strong period now, thanks to effective management and a keen community spirit of ballplaying in southern Maine and New England generally. Back in the 1970's a six-team league generated quite a bit of interest locally with good competition that featured a fixed number of mercenaries; each team could carry three "ringers" from outside Portland on its roster. One can imagine the abuses that led to that legislation, but it resulted in a form of league parity that made championships mean something.

Then as now, the toughest battle is often the one just to get on a decent field. Through all its years the Twilight has competed outside itself for access to the best ballyards. Administrators of city-owned fields tend to favor the city youth leagues — Legion and Babe Ruth baseball — and so getting permits to use city parks like Deering Oaks becomes tough. When the best fields are out of reach, leagues resort to whatever the local earth offers up. Fields can be very good or very bad. Community fields may be unkempt — no lines, the infield dirt not screened for rocks or dragged smooth, the turf possibly unmowed — unless some local greenman saint sees otherwise. Under most circumstances players do some field work to get games in, bending their backs to laborer's tasks then playing a Sunday twi-night doubleheader, the first seven-inning game starting at 5:30, then the nightcap at 8. It goes late. Twilight comes early, and so does Monday.

◆

Now comprised of roughly eighty percent college players (many from Division-I schools, including the baseball powerhouse University of Maine Bears at Orono, just to the north) the league has lots of young and strong and well-coached players, a changing mix of them from year to year. But there's also a number of older guys — roughly twenty percent of the league are guys in their late twenties and thirties. They make the league happen. The kids come and go, play two-three years, that's it. But a core of oldtimers keeps the Twilight League from fading away. And this mix creates a solid level of play; a Twilight all-star team could compete well against NCAA Division-I baseball teams, even lacking the advantage of everyday play.

Some of the older players are perennial sluggers. Many play into their thirties, some into their forties and a few past fifty. They play — that is, they compete on par with the young studs, the meat-sticks. Simple dignity dictates that you leave the game before you hang shame; but some of these guys never seem to hang, and so never leave. A young Colby College player in the Twilight described being struck by the intensity and devotion of the older guys, and trying to step up his game to show them he could really play. The old guys relate a Twilight truism: "You don't win with kids." Meaning, teams with a solid core of veteran players tend to prevail come playoff time, showing their kids how to take the game all the way through to the end. Without that knowing core, young teams are shown the what-for by the first band of wily-and-agile elders they meet.

♦

Gary Dube ("Doobie") is a meat stick (now a league official) going with a graceful intensity into his mid-thirties. He was my contact — his name had been in the news article that first made me aware of the league. I tracked him down and had breakfast with him at a lovely old diner in South Portland, where we drank some coffee and told stories. He and the other "old guys" spend the long winter talking about the coming season, ones just past, and more of the same. And they work winter-long to keep muscle, breathing game history as a living text amongst their families, friends and mates. It was fun to tap into that over eggs and toast with a diner's rattle and hum as a backdrop.

The playing stakes can be high for a workingman. You go for broke on Sunday then crawl into work on Monday. Those doing physical labor are most affected by injury and fatigue, but everyone who plays feels it; even if you're sitting at a desk, you're gulping aspirin to keep the pain dogs at bay. One Twilight pitcher is a commercial fisherman, and as Gary says, he's a different fisherman on Monday morning than he is with a few days rest. The fish don't jump into the boat when you're dragging a sore leg. Life's other battles are fed by the game even as they're bled by it.

As Gary relates it, the Twilight story is a strong one — a restoration tale with the happiest ending, which is no ending. The fair publicity arises from the fact that it's good baseball — a solid league that's made itself work for the betterment of the local game. In recent seasons three issues — high-tech alloy bats, league finances and competitive parity — have driven new policies that are proving effective in giving the Twilight new life.

In the first case, with new alloy bats gaining currency across amateur leagues has come a frightening increase in sheer dumb hitting. With a sweet spot that covers most of the bat, the new alloys make it possible to hit checked-swing doubles and handcuffed singles. Pitchers face line-drive comebackers that explode off the bat like gunshots; even medium-good hitters are capable of hitting killer line drives with the new weaponry. Most pitchers do not fare well or develop confidence under that kind of fire.

The Twilight League went back to wooden bats in 1996. This mandate streamlined the game, distilling it back to its original form. Significantly, a wood bat forces a hitter to really hit. The sweet spot on a wooden bat is small — a mere few inches on the fat of the barrelhead — and if a batter's swinging at fastballs busting him inside, he's breaking his gamer again. A wood bat is a real bat that delivers real hits, making the hitter master a more rigorous discipline, rewarding pitchers that make good pitches and keep batters off-balance. Now Twilight games go by faster. There are fewer lost balls. Pitchers throw strikes, and the best hitters still hit. It's truer baseball.

Teams now spend a bit more of their budget on their bat supply, because wooden bats do break, but finally the players are responsible for replenishing the inventory. That first year, hitters (and pitchers) chewed through dozens of bats; now, more hitters have learned how to hit with wood, and they don't break so many. Fact is, when aluminum bats were in, most teams had many more than they actually used. Now, a workingman player buys his own $18 gamer, and if he breaks it, he buys another.

Such basic discipline is also working its way with league finances. A "pay-to-play" system now relies upon the players to fund their own seasons, breaking (or at least lessening) teams' dependency upon sponsor money. Local sponsors— small retail businesses, body shops, bars, boutiques— are hit upon by everyone from the peewee leagues to the over-thirties, as well as little girls' softball teams. No way can they fully fund all ages, shapes and sizes of local ball. In the past, serious teams with ongoing financial backing from a sugar-daddy sponsor enjoyed distinct advantages and a clear competitive edge. There's never enough sponsorship money to go around, so the moneyed teams become monsters, cutting through their local leagues like chainsaws, year after year. The parallels to current financial disparities in the Majors are compelling; with a limited pool of surpassing talent at any level, the rich get richer and the others tend to become mere fodder — unless they somehow manage to win. Which they sometimes do.

The Twilight League's new pay-to-play system redefines the formula: each team has to come up with four thousand dollars for the season, and they now do it mainly by charging players a roster fee. This was a defining initiative of the MSBL on Long Island, and is a key distinction between the "semipro" ball of yore and what is now more strictly amateur baseball. In semipro ball, companies, unions, clubs, and sometimes local syndicates financed teams and leagues— not just in Twilight, but everywhere semipro was played. With those interests funding the show, all sorts of manipulations of rules, rosters and ringers flavored seasons and favored powerhouse teams to dominate local scenes for years on end. It's not a formula for widespread delight among the other far-flung teams, players, families and fans of the marginal game. These perennial also-rans enjoyed little hope week after week and year after year of beating the one or two best teams. In this sort of situation, losing is toxic; the marginal teams struggle year-to-year simply to continue, and not die out. Meanwhile, for the strong teams, too many games are a cakewalk and thus bear more than trace poison even in winning.

In the Twilight, pay-to-play balances the equation in a decisive and democratic way. Money paid by each player — typically around $200 for a season —finances field rentals, insurance, night-game lights, umpires, baseballs and all the other necessities. Living within the limits of what those fees can afford, the League stands on its own.

Paying to play clearly underlines amateur status and normalizes the equation among a broad pool of players. In a practical sense, it's the best demonstration of a player's desire, making it easy for coaches to know who they can count upon to be there come game time. While money is still sometimes put to service in assuring the best players play, college players have to avoid obvious incentives to protect their NCAA eligibility, and coaches, for the most part, toe the line.

But even more than clearing the financial house, enhancing competitive parity with a draft system has saved the soul of the Twilight.

For years, the dominant teams were clearly attractive to the best new players, and had complete power to control their rosters. They kept whatever current players they wanted, and brought new ones onto the roster at will. The depth of their talent made them locally unbeatable. Now, an annual league draft mandates that each team can protect only eight roster players for the first round each winter. All unprotected roster players are up for grabs by other teams for the following season. A team can protect ten players and skip a draft round, or protect twelve and skip two rounds, but in the process other teams pick up all the best new talent. Standing pat while the balance shifts elsewhere in the league can lead to some surprising competition; it lets teams take a run with more than their core intact, going up against fresh teams each year. But no team stands pat for long; most of the college players cycle out in a few seasons anyway.

The draft system promotes continuous talent flow through the league and its even distribution among teams. To compete for the best new players, teams surrender rights to current ones they'd otherwise keep. From the players' side, if you're not protected you can be claimed by another Twilight team, and must play for them if you play in the league at all. If you're not drafted, you can compete for a roster spot on your present team — up against the core of protected players plus whatever new talent has arrived via the draft.

The MSBL leagues tend to use more open and voluntary roster systems. There are no required roster-defining drafts; players are free to switch teams from season to season. Open drafts are held, but the league doesn't force teams to participate. It's strictly voluntary, and if a team is looking for some new players, they can come to an open workout to take a look. There's still a fair amount of player movement between teams, but it's by the free choice of a player and a team, with few if any restrictions. Naturally, teams commit to final rosters by a certain date during the season, so most of this shuffling takes place between seasons—in Maine as elsewhere, beside hot stoves.

As a player, I hopped from the Stony Brook Cardinals to the Brentwood Yanquis to the Oyster Bay Bombers over a ten-season span in Long Island's MSBL and MABL. I switched teams as new opportunities presented themselves, and liked having such freedom within that baseball culture. But playing within the strictures of the Twilight draft system ups the ante, firming the competitive boundaries to make the enterprise more challenging athletically—still amateur, but with higher stakes and a stronger pulse. Whether playing simply to play or to find the highest edge you can reach, wooden bats, pay-to-play and the draft systems define the challenges more clearly, requiring real resolve to go for it, all out.

Smart moves bring winners in from the twilight. Playing for a season in that league with those guys—and the gloaming—could be a lovely capstone, a good place to end up.

Townball

One of the damndest things about my two years of Kenyon baseball was the fact that almost no one on the team played summer ball. This astounded me. Here were these kids with starting spots on a college roster who'd go home each summer and play tennis and golf, but no baseball? Simply astonishing. When I'd ask them about it, they'd blink: Baseball? At home? In the summer? It made me wonder where they came from; I pictured Europe — hedge-rows hiding long Belgian Block driveways and luxuriously-vacant homes. The dolor of privileged angst, with the means to go anywhere and nowhere to go. Whatever the real scene was, they surely weren't diving for grounders in a home-sweet-home summer sweat.

Now, things are different for the Lords. At new coach Matt Burdette's urging they all find summer teams, reporting back to Kenyon each fall better at something than when they left. And its no wonder that Lew's best player — Kenyon's best player — is part of a present dynasty back home in Minnesota, playing what they call Townball.

Mitch Swaggert's summertime Minnesota ballplaying carries the deep resonance of another game called townball, a forerunner of baseball played in the mid-nineteenth century. Nowadays, wooly teams all around the country recreate early versions of vintage townball under various sets of rules dating from 1845 to 1927. There's even a league that plays a full summer schedule at the Old Bethpage Village Restoration on Long Island, many of its players supplementing their amateur MSBL ballplaying with showcase townball in front of eager weekend crowds, just down the old lane from period-costumed shopkeepers, quiltmakers and blacksmiths. They play the old game for real, wearing vintage woolen uniforms but real baseball spikes. The only glove allowed is a plain leather workglove with the fingers cut off. Such tiny gloves barely lessen the sting of the hard, heavy homemade ball, and the most devoted players eschew them. Their hearty handshakes feature all manner of bent and broken fingers.

Townball teams around the country (often affiliated with regional museums and historical societies) play under various sets of rules that are carefully researched and faithfully enforced. The 1866 game features underhanded pitching, flyballs caught on one bounce are outs, and you can hurl the ball at a baserunner to "soak" him for an out. Under 1877 rules, pitching is overhanded and the game picks up speed and ferocity. Teams don't score runs, they cross aces. The "ballists" throw hard and their play is "plucky." A batter gets four strikes, and five balls to walk; a foul ball is not counted as a strike, but a foul tip caught by the catcher on any pitch is a "hand down" out. Early Victorian manners are part of the deal, so the umpire levies fines for swearing while encouraging use of 1860s idiolect. Cries of "What the blazes!" and "Smite it!" curry favor and add to the flavor. Proper handshakes are likewise cherished, while high-fives are given the eye. It's living history, remarkable for how powerfully it can transport players and crowds into another sense of time and place.

◆

Mitch Swaggert and the Minnesota boys don't play any vintage anything. Their townball is hard-nosed, rigorous baseball played in the postmodern manner. The Minnesota State Amateur League (organized under the Minnesota Baseball Association) is a statewide league organized by town, with A, B & C levels mapped to town populations. The league's been going since 1926, and now comprises 50 big-town

Class-A teams, another 48 in small-town Class-B, and 150 rural Class-C teams. The only roster restriction is geographic; a player can belong to a team more than 25 miles from his home only if he first secures a League waiver with clear reason.

The fact that teams are geographically ruled, restricted to locals, means that teams can take anyone of their ilk. Towns tend to have (and want to have) good teams, investing them with a fair share of civic pride. The town ballparks are kept up nicely, as a rule, in this same Minnesota reflex. There are many fine ballfields all across the state — sparkling small-city parks and old-town classics hosting hometown teams. There is special pride in the old stadiums with their wooden grandstands, the game kept true with manicured infields and serene facings. The outfield fences carry a layered record of the long march of local commerce — realtors, insurance agents, car dealers, Coca-Cola. Modern-day Minnesota townball is living history recreated in the present tense with time passing under fair northern summertime skies.

Mitch plays in Minnetonka Mills for the Millers of the Riverview League. Their home field is Big Willow Park, a city-run ballpark that hosts Legion ball along with townball. The Millers have won the State Class-A Championship three years in a row now, and they've been a power team for longer than that. They've worked their way to the top over the past five seasons with a second-place finish, then a third, then three championships. They play four games a week, mostly weeknights with some Sundays mixed in. Games start at 8 P.M., but sometimes earlier if a home team doesn't have a lit field.

Minnesota's *Ball Diamond News* is published six times a year, monthly from May to October, in Spring Park. Its masthead asserts that "the focus is Amateur Baseball and is targeted to all baseball participants from age eight and up." Their May '98 issue, loaned to me by Kevin Hoy, has a brief Millers history: "The Minnetonka Millers joined the Riverview League of Class A Minnesota Amateur Baseball in 1976. For the first 4 years they were known as the Tonka Bottle Shop. In 1981 Kevin Hoy took over the team as a player-coach-general manager and changed the name.... The team has primarily consisted of current and former college players that live in or close to Minnetonka, or graduated from Minnetonka. The Millers have posted Riverview Championships in 1977-79, 1983-84, 1989, and 1993-97. Their team colors are

Royal, Grey and Black. In recent history the Millers have been one of the most dominant teams in the state, posting 5 Riverview titles, one third-place state finish, two second-place state finishes and one State Championship in the last five years. The Millers play between 45-50 games per summer. Most of the non-league play is against the top-level Class A and B teams throughout the state. The present team boats a roster of all present or former Division-I, II or III college players, three of which have played minor league ball after their college careers."

◆

As in Maine's Twilight League, the winning teams find a solid mix of young and older players, featuring young college studs along with guys in their mid-twenties to mid-thirties, and a few older. The mix is key. "You don't win with kids" is what they say in Maine; "the teams that win have older players" is the Minnesota chestnut. Crafty veterans bring the winning intangibles to the campaign — knowledge and long-game chops mixed with a pinch of come-from-behind magic. They know how to brew up a win in any weather.

The geographic rosters seem to foster parity at all the levels, and fierce competition at the championships. In almost 80 years, only one team has won Class A three times in row — Mitch's Millers. They feature a cast of players who are some of the best in the state, a few of whom have gotten better past their thirtieth birthday. Their 31-year-old pitcher Brian Krull has won the league MVP award twice as they've marched to the final weekend, through sectionals to the state championship games. As a team, they climbed the steps of getting better until they were best, finally ready to win it all after knocking on the door for several seasons. Sunday, Tuesday, Wednesday and Friday, they come to play and win.

Kevin Hoy sent me a calendar — also published by the folks at *Ball Diamond News*— featuring aerial beauty shots of some of Minnesota townball's best ballparks. The grace of those diamonds speaks volumes for how the game is played upon them. The calendar includes loving landscapes of Parade Stadium, a baseball cathedral since 1907 with the Minneapolis skyline now filling the entire panorama beyond the outfield hedges; Brainerd's Don Adamson Field, the home of the Warriors with its stolid green wooden fences; Waseca's Tink Larson Field, impeccably groomed with grandstand seats recovered from the demolition of Metropolitan Stadium, the original home of the Minnesota Twins; Chaska Athletic Park, built by the people of Chaska in 1950 and financed by the issuance of $50-per-share stock; Memorial Park in Fairfax with its huge left field and white barn grandstand; Johnson Field in New Ulm, site of the 1953 State Amateur Tournament where the championship game was played before 31,031 fans; and Sleepy Eye Baseball Park with farm fields in deep dead left and right, a tiny grandstand and acres of standing room.

Kevin also sent the Minnesota Baseball Association 2000 Handbook, which boldly advertises this year's state tournament in Sleepy Eye, home of the Class C Sleepy Eye Indians. The annual Handbook is a sweet little series of 5.5" by 3.65" booklets, simply but professionally produced by Perfection Printing in Norwood. Each bears the names and numbers of all the league officers, directors and regional commissioners; all 14 articles of the league constitution; the high school player restrictions; and a code of ethics that begins with "baseball is played by gentlemen," continues with "umpires ... should be as inconspicuous as possible while handling a ballgame" and ends with "give the best you have!" The rest of the book comprises full-page ads from league sponsors like Belgrade Livestock, announcing "WANTED TO BUY — Butcher Cows — Lame, Lazy or Thin — Dairy Herds, Young Stock — also Fats. Dairy or Beef Bulls for Sale or Rent." Towards the back of the Handbook you'll find a listing of State Champions from 1924 onward and the prior year's All-Tournament Team (1999's includes no less than six Minnetonka Millers). The Minnesota Amateur Baseball Hall of Fame follows with the names of the original 1963 members followed by each intervening year's selections, usually four to five per season. League MVP awards dating from 1938 are next, then the state tournament attendance records (10,981 last year in Granite Falls and Marshall, over 1,100 for the final game). The last two pages list the Brennan Sportsmanship Trophy winners since 1941 (this is a team trophy) and the individual players who have won the Mike Downes Memorial Award, inaugurated in 1981.

◆

The kingpin amateur baseball league East of the Mississippi is the Cape Cod League, and it deserves more than a mention — it could be its own book. Cape Cod is the premiere wood-bat league in the east, drawing the very best D-I college players from across the nation and Central America. One of its teams, the Orleans Cardinals, publishes its own annual Reference Book and Photo Album, and the 1997 Reference Book features three full pages of former Cape Cod players currently in the majors. It also has a centerfold photo spread with Eldridge Park in the foreground and Nauset Beach in the eastern distance, beyond which rides the mighty Atlantic. It's classic baseball, right at our nation's first edge.

The Cape Cod League may be the most celebrated amateur baseball league, but Minnesota townball is a mainstay. Its consistency and authenticity are hard to beat, you bet. Townball players bring their best and leave it all on the field, without a doubt. I'd not survive the first cut — certainly not in A.

Game Face

Jim Crow was a pre–Civil War minstrel character, a caricature Negro played by white comics and singers with blackened faces in wagon-borne touring shows. What came to be called Jim Crow after that ghastly war was a shadowy description of American apartheid, the institutional racism both public and private, apparent and hidden, whose residues still plague us today.

Long after slavery's abolition in the U.S., many whites continued to regard blacks as inherently inferior. All sorts of religious and pseudo-scientific rationalizations were created to support this view in the Jim Crow era, with the U.S. Supreme Court giving legal validity to official white supremacism — in 1883 declaring the Civil Rights Act of 1875 unconstitutional, and in 1896 legitimizing the principle of "separate but equal" in *Plessy v. Ferguson.* These decisions fostered a slew of so-called Jim Crow laws in the southern states; by 1914 every state below the Mason-Dixon line had legislated societal separation, black from white. Distinct facilities figured a shadow civilization within the U.S. — separate schools most explicitly, and public transit (back of the bus), and restaurants, and washrooms, and drinking fountains. Separate churches and cemeteries. Separate sets of rules for public behavior, with the private behavior of blacks made public with deadly force when it encountered the wrong white men in the wrong place and time.

Baseball was never exempt, and sadly couldn't lead us out of the dark. Jim Crow banished the few blacks who were playing pro around 1900, and kept the game all-white at most professional levels until well after the Second World War — which is to say, we figured out nuclear fission before we figured out race. It's a complex system, sadly beyond us in many ways still. Blacks were barred from baseball's limelight for a long, long time, although from time to time owners and managers tried passing off talented black players as Cubans or American Indians to get them on their teams. Baseball's touring character — the bright local venues and the traveling road — had the same showtime quality as the old minstrels, enforcing popular beliefs in its depiction of an elevated all-white national pastime. Big league white ballplayers had the grace of opportunity in their own time. Negroes were for light entertainment. The game held them off until 1948, when Jackie Robinson was allowed to test Jim Crow's cruelty, proving its tragic insanity and besting it. By the year I was born, 1953, there were a total of 20 black men playing on seven of the sixteen major league teams.

Today, many of baseball's biggest stars are black men, and a wave of Latino and Asian immigrants are adding new talent to the big league game. The amateur trenches have always been more open to racial mixing and testing, with open racial competition taking place on a personal level. Having had a taste of that, I can testify that it cuts both ways now, and always has. The Bombers were a very solidly multiracial team, in my era; on the field we were colorless but for our black uniforms and ancestors. The old black men who came to see us play had beaten Whitey Ford in his time, before he got to the bigs. Imagine. What was the atmosphere like for those games, with black teams going up against the whites just at the end of Jim Crow — or what we like to think of as its end — with the door now open to the bigs? One can imagine some hard-fought ballgames, many black Bomber victories, and some settling and unsettling of the question.

Now, Hispanics are coming on strong. In playing with the Yanquis and against Carlos and his Dominicans I did battle alongside them for their place in the culture via baseball, and served some time as a minority myself. I experienced the pushback of what's called reverse racism, but is really just racism, too. It's a canker, and has nothing to do with the game. We'd best get over it soon. And will we ever?

♦

The Negro Leagues Museum at Eighteenth and Vine in Kansas City has at its center a small green-carpeted diamond inhabited by life-sized bronzes of some all-time great, Jim Crow–era black ballplayers. These guys played an ecstatic brand of ball in a league of their own, one whose spirit is only hinted-at now in places such as this. These black men were professional working ballplayers who, in their time and milieu, brought the game to a higher level of spirited skill in front of dazzled crowds. Barred from Major League Baseball and the professional minor leagues by segregation, black ballplayers created a spectacular "shadow" game with a radiant flavor never bested in the bigs, and only approximated in the very best semipro hometown showdowns. If there's one damnable thing about the integration of Major League Baseball it was the near-immediate disappearance of the Negro Leagues, shadowball, and the understanding those local crowds had of what was going on.

Eighteenth and Vine is a museum now — the whole block seems glass-cased. The Jazz Museum occupies the same renovated building as the Negro League Museum, with the restored Gem Theater across the street, buffed to a shine. Neighborhood stores are now vacant, but for their lovingly-sanitized front windows stocked with depression-era goods. It's ghostly, in a curated sort of way. In its heyday, this neighborhood was a nexus for so much cultural glory — the jazz, the ballplayers — and such life — everyone decked out in their finest on Saturday night, huge crowds coming down Sunday after church to cheer for the boys — and it's all very gone now, as a lone car creeps down the block and its driver takes a nervous glance at me on the sidewalk.

But inside the museum life comes up closer — a sarcophagus holding a whole host of players cast in bronze. To get what's going on within this scaled-down diamond, you have to look into the eyes of these statues; you have to recognize where each of them is looking to understand that there is a game going on here, and these guys are playing. You can see in their stillness the sure wisdom they had in knowing where they were, where they stood, and how to play this game. Whoever cast them knew something. These guys are wearing game faces.

Satchel Paige is on the mound, and he's gazing in at the plate with his body erect yet poised and his feet apart — like a lithe cat about to pounce. His face belies nothing — a batter is watching. Josh Gibson is his catcher, and they seem locked in to each other as if listening to the same radio show, even as Gibson surveys his infield. Walter "Buck" Leonard is at first base, holding a moment of tactical eye contact with Ray Dandridge at third. Seeing them here, each acknowledging the other's part in the scheme, brings a momentary echo to this hushed center of the museum — as if a huge boisterous crowd is holding its breath. John Henry "Pop" Lloyd stands straight and alert at second base, and at shortstop "Judy" Johnson (William, by birth) leans forward to read Josh Gibson's posture and lips, to know what's coming next. From left field to right, James "Cool Papa" Bell, Oscar Charleston and Leon Day are spread out like birds about to take flight upon an imminent rifle-crack. Martin Dihigo is stepping up to bat, and he's ready, he thinks, for what Satchell can bring to him now. The moment is seized, but pulsing. It's easy to imagine the whole crew shifting into high gear in pursuit of a little white ball — easy to see the flight of these lifelike bronzes, tragic in their absolute stillness.

Andrew "Rube" Foster, who founded and ran the Negro Leagues from this very neighborhood, stands watching the whole scene as if he owns it. And he does. Buck O'Neill is managing from the sidelines, soaking in the whole tableaux to remake into spoken jazz, later. The scene is complete, and yet never again so. A team of artisans at Oxbow Foundry in Lawrence, Kansas, cast these men and this moment as a rich, but finally scant reminder of what once was, what the game could be in truth and despite all injustice. It's a shadow of one branch of the larger game, long banished and now, too late, quietly celebrated. This game had a face, and its look was full of all the living color that could possibly be.

Hurt

Often the second day is the worst. You play on Sunday, firing all of your bullets, and you wake up Monday feeling groggy, hazy, dehydrated. It's very much like a hangover, the older you get. You drift all through Monday with frayed aching edges, but it's not until Tuesday that you really hurt. By Wednesday you're getting over it; come Thursday you're no longer thirsty and your juices are flowing to do it again.

Playing hurt is a part of the deal for everyone, because you can't not get hurt in this game, at least a little hurt. Carrying aches and pains is routine, and until they're severe enough to intrude absolutely you can block them out for gametime, not even feeling them consciously. What your body is doing to process those signals out is another complex system in place, humming along to get the job done. You can put injury away for a time and pay the price later — a hell of a good deal, if you think about it.

But injury has a way of sneaking up on you. Fostered by fatigue and by an accumulation of small nicks, an injury can manifest out of a leaping dive, or a hard collision on the bases, or simply taking an awkward swing. Basketball brought me my first torn ankle, but I reinjured it stepping off a curb, distracted in Manhattan. Hurt takes hold at inopportune moments, changing the course of the river. You can get down on yourself, ashamed of your new incapacity and banishment. And a dirty little secret is true of most coaches: they get mad at you when you get hurt. Their anger is a residue of disappointment, and thus is factored heavily by how good you are — if you're really good, or they think you are, they get really mad. They can hate you for getting hurt. The best ones don't, but there aren't many of those.

Once you're discounted as injured, you're off the set in a very real sense. Out of the lineup. No role to play. You become sort of invisible, in a creepy way. It drives some players to distraction, especially when a coach loads fuel on that wet fire then pisses it out to remind you that you no longer count, forcing bitter refuge in what could have been.

What's remarkable to experience is the body's power to heal, to come back even stronger. Depending on the injury, strengths may have to shift in compensation. But they do. Somehow your body figures out how to do it another way. You can put away the residues of pain in a knee or ribcage and go at the game as hard as you ever did.

My ankles have long plagued me — I tore the right one my senior year in high school, then the left one while rehabbing. Those injuries took me out of the game for a long time, but not forever. The worst injury, in terms of sheer pain, was the shoulder tear I suffered a few years back. I knew exactly when I hurt it, but had no real pain for almost two weeks — just a feeling of weakness and a slight sense of displacement. Then I awoke one night in agony, pinned to the bed with the shoulder feeling blasted. A doctor found muscle tears and suggested a cortisone shot to ease the inflammation — to which I quickly agreed, having not slept well in a week. He inserted a long needle deep into my shoulder socket and slowly dripped the cortisone in there. Anyone who has ever had one of these will be grimacing now. It worked — in a couple days, the pain was but a lingering trace.

But I had no strength, at first. I tried throwing empty-handed and could barely make the motion. Balled-up socks were next; I found I could toss them barely ten feet to the livingroom wall. It was pathetic.

Along with the shot the doctor had given me a Thera-band — an elastic rubber hose for rehab exercises. I tied one end to the refrigerator door handle and pulled easy arm extensions — straight up from the hip, straight out to the side, and up at angles. I got in the habit of doing reps every time I walked past the fridge. Weeks of this mindless routine began to show results — I was doing full windups now and throwing sock changeups with some authority. I began lifting light hand-weights, doing lots of reps of those same Thera-band motions. The three-pound weights felt heavy at first, but soon got lighter. The livingroom rug became a mound, a place to stand and prepare to throw. And I began putting myself to sleep by imagining that view from the hill, and the paths the body takes to bring a tough strike to the plate.

At this stage — with thought working everything out — I began feeling power again, and balance, and all of the urge to play. It was as if I was regaining mass, finding potential right there where I'd left it. I was praying in an active way — envisioning what was to come. Seeing my own deliverance back to the sacred ground of real game. Praying to play.

Prayers are sometimes answered. It's a hell of a deal.

More or Less

The gap between amateur ball and the pros has a lot to do with frequency of playing time, and not having another livelihood supporting the play. Pro players' play supports itself. As a weekend warrior, you can go a full week of days between games, even as you do your other work to make a living. You try to find ways to keep an edge. It's harder to carry momentum from game to game with such long insistent pauses.

There are guys who just show up and excel, regardless of how much time has passed since their last game. Chuck O'Donnell was one such. An NHL official, Chuck would go for half a summer without playing baseball, then George would call him up and coax him down, and Chuck would put on his Cardinal uni and strap on the catching gear, throw out three runners stealing and hit two home runs. No length of time, it seemed, was enough to diminish his timing, his eye or his fire. Coming off a year-long layoff, he'd suit up and lead the charge, nonchalant-like. We lesser mortals would work the season long for what Chuck could pull out of his back pocket.

Back in our Cardinal days, Rosie and I did extra midweek workouts to build endurance and fine-tune our timing. Toward the season's end, with the MSBL Phoenix tournament looming, we'd up the frequency and pace of those workouts, and when we got to Arizona and those jeweled fields the extra work paid off in bright silver dollars. Many guys didn't prepare that way, making the leap from once-a-week games to daily tournament doubleheaders, sagging early and getting hurt.

With daily play, even for just a week like in Phoenix, you have baseball as real religion, just like the priests. Every day has its rituals. Food and sleep become precious. Pulling on the socks before each game is like dressing to celebrate services. There's a reflective echo before and after each win and loss, bracketing the sacraments of game. When other chores and cares drop away — no job to report to, no buttons to punch — and the game's graces are all that immediately matter, you find the full absorption in play that resides at the very heart of it. Understood that way, on that frequency, the amateur game gets a glimpse of the true calling, making its mark of authentic presence in a player's prayer — his daily play.

Again

Baseball predictions are about as dependable as weather forecasts. In the game as in the atmosphere, the complexity of the system offers too many variables for certainty in foretelling. Players and teams find ways to surpass expectations and fall short of them, to beat the odds and suffer them, day by day. Sizing it up from the sidelines requires a lot of cognitive sense, the ability to discern fine differences in performance, and faith in intuitive knowing. Scouts, coaches and bird dogs all do it their own way, and the results of their judgments gather like hurricane and like drought.

There's lots of voodoo infused in pitching, but some guys just go out there and get it done. Hitting likewise. But there's no universal correct way to do either. Different approaches work for different players. And for both hitters and pitchers, this is also true: the best players do certain things the same way. Those who prevail over the long run strive to do them the same way every time, with monkish discipline and faith in results.

"Same way every time" doesn't mean robotically. The crux of success in baseball lies in making fine adjustments. A hitter has to adjust constantly to what a pitcher is throwing, pitch by pitch. One who sits back waiting for the same pitch against a good pitcher will seldom see it and most often trudge back to the dugout with his head hanging. And a pitcher who throws the same way every time — same speed, same location, same movement or lack of movement — will get hammered in kind, finding safety only on the bench.

So these two opposing skill sets— pitching and hitting — are bound in the same orbit, feeding off each other or starving. They share a common baseball condition: to succeed they have to wobble a bit, adjusting their spin in active ways to ride the ball forward. For all such adjustments, consistency remains vital. The best players find ways to adapt without essentially changing the rote mechanics of their approach.

A hitter who toys with his stance and swing during real at-bats will really struggle. A pitcher experimenting with his delivery during real innings will fail to put quality pitches around the strikezone with any consistency. In either case, failure dogs the player and the game runs him to ground.

Same way every time is thus both a constant goal and an elusive one. The real goal is to win, and one wins by expressing power over and over again, surpassing opposing expressions. With hitting, it's a matter of keeping the hands back, the head down, and the eyes steady on the ball. It's feeling the fat part of the bat as an extension of your hands, knowing where that bat-head is in the same way that you know where your fingers are, or the point of your chin — thoughtlessly. With all of the possible variations in taking a good strong hack at a baseball, those elements are there — the hands held back for the moment that the torso turns in the swing. If the hands are ahead of that turn, bat hits ball before the power transfers; if the hands lag behind the power shift, the result is a slow bat, and foul pops the opposite way. But if the hands — the wrists and lower arms — extend at just the moment that the legs and hips torque, just the moment when the ball spins into the hitting zone, then even an easy swing (a swing that feels easy) can deliver a long-gone shot.

For pitchers, it's a matter of keeping the front shoulder closed just a moment longer than what feels easy and natural. Turning that shoulder open too soon spends the body's power on nothing; the front shoulder links to the throwing arm, just across the way. If that shoulder rotates and the throwing arm lags behind, it'll move through the arm slot with a fraction of its possible power. Here again, getting the fine timing right — keeping that front shoulder in until the arm starts through the slot — brings all the power of the body to bear on the pitch. Even a small guy with a narrow body can generate power pitches if he has his shoulder action in sync. Because you don't pitch with your arm, you pitch with your body. And if body and soul find this power rhythm, good pitches become as regular as religion and as right as rain.

From either side of the equation — pitching or hitting — mechanics vary. Players find all sorts of ways to deliver on the promise. The key ingredient is purpose. All throwing relates to a game; all swings in the cage, in batting practice, and in the on-deck circle focus on getting it right in the moment that counts. That is a point that does not wobble. Past is prologue, and you practice in the present for the future. It all matters. You do it now to do it (better) again.

Ballyards

Each is particular. Each has its place. I keep an emotional slideshow of them, more felt than seen, each with specific muscle memories holding its moment intact. Each one has a trace of me, more here than there in the larger scheme of things. These ballyards had my moment in a long swirl of many others. My time upon them was brief; their time upon me stays.

◆

State was what it was— our first blessed homefield, our stadium mind. It was the place that gave us baseball's sense of enclosed-yet-boundless possibility — the enclosures physical, the boundlessness all spirit.

This ribbon of state land was— is— a slender valley dug out to create an elevated highway hillside back when the Long Island suburbs were just forming up. Along the top of the state hill runs the parkway that brought my nuclear family here from Queens in 1954. Drainage culverts feed into State at this corner, where the parkway passes over Union Street, the train tracks, and a smaller road called Orinoco.

Our corner of State was all spare-parts ballpark — dugouts dug out of the sandy clay, a small flat-topped pine tree for our broadcast booth, the right-field hill perfect bleachers with a home-run line marked by discarded two-by-fours laid end-to-end. Left field featured the mattresses dumped over backyard fences by the arrivistes; we propped them up in a line to figure the deep left and left-center walls.

Defined by what surrounded it, State was the neighborhood ballpark, all homemade and all real. An easy walk and a vault over the back fence and there you were. A blind old hotdog man kept his cart just a few yards up Union Street, under the overpass. He was our biggest fan. Cops and road workers would park atop the right-field bleachers to watch us play for free, but the paying crowds were in our heads. Complete.

Brentwood's Danny Hommel Field was our home for Gorilla softball. A large electrical tower looms over short right field, and one night a druggy kid hung himself upside-down from his legs near the top of the tower and howled the whole game. We pegged pebbles at him to try to shut him up, but he was still up there jabbering when the game ended.

Danny Hommel's dirt infield is pitted with potholes. The pitcher's mound is inverted — an actual depression — so you have to step up to deliver a pitch. The backstop is rusted and bent, with sections of chain link mangled as if chewed by monsters. The surrounding streets are unfamiliar, so after a game we walk in a group back to our cars with bats at the ready. But the only fights are routine brawls that break out on the field, usually settled without much bloodshed. Suz comes to watch us play one night and says she's never seen a game like that.

We wonder who Danny Hommel was, figuring him for a neighborhood kid who died before his time. But we never really knew.

◆

Nassau County's Bay Park has a decent, well-maintained grass infield but a shaggy outfield — balls sometimes get lost in the thick, shin-high grass. The field sits right beside Jamaica Bay, and we play there mostly at night under the lights with a wind blowing in from left.

One evening, with severe thunderstorms gathering over the greater metropolitan area, a police car with its lights rolling creeps slowly down the walkway in the middle of an inning. A cop's booming voice broadcasts this dire warning over the loudspeaker: something to the effect of, tornadoes in the area — remain at your own risk. Lightning is flicking the edges of the horizon as the game pauses to look around.

No sooner does the cop drive off than this bagpipe band comes marching down that same path, wailing a ghostly battle hymn in Highland airs. It's the Brotherhood of Electrical Workers, practicing parade maneuvers. They spook the shit out of the umpires, who call the game and take off running.

We pack up and haul our gear back to the cars with lightning flying all around us, and as we drive off, we watch the electricians cradling their bagpipes beneath the big trees, right where our mothers had long ago told us they shouldn't have been.

◆

The State University at Stony Brook diamond was one of the better ones around, and George managed to secure it as our Cardinal home field.

Stony Brook had all the accouterments of a good ballpark but was poorly maintained by the college maintenance crew. We once drove my old truck up onto the infield to drag it before a game; a security officer spotted us and threatened to pull our permit. No vehicles on the field, gentlemen.

But the thick woods behind the backstop and down the right-field line were its biggest drawback — we lost foul balls in there by the dozens. The woods were infested with deer ticks and everyone was afraid of getting Lyme disease. But we had to recover some of those balls, so we held a vote and chose a scrub, wrapped him in a tarpaulin and duct tape, and sent him in. He looked like a spectre of death, only bright blue, and he came out with a bucket full. Afterwards, as he itched on the bench, we all scratched.

On another Sunday, some friends from work came to watch me play, and right after they left I hit the deepest home run of my life over the left-field fence, over the service road, and into the waste treatment plant. On Monday I told them what they'd missed. I don't think they believed me, but that's the old ballgame.

◆

Tempe Diablo Stadium: it's as if we've died and gone to baseball heaven. The autumn Phoenix air is warm and dry, so dry that your sweat evaporates instantly — your skin doesn't even know you're sweating. After sagging through our first tournament, we learn to pound water to stave off dehydration.

Rosie gallops across that scenic green outfield like a wild pony; Goldy gathers grounders at third like he's roping doggies. The rocky buttes in deep left make us all strut like Hollywood cowboys and play like the bright southwestern stars we are.

◆

Smithtown's Flynn Park: some long-lost pal of Goldy's strolls up one night and recognizes him. The two of them have a little reunion behind the backstop, chattering old times when, all of a sudden, the game freezes. It's Goldy's turn at bat, and where the hell is he? With a sheepish grin he snakes around the fencing, hops into the batter's box and tips the bill of his helmet in a quick apology to the umpire.

Barely set in the box, he belts the first pitch clear out of the park in left-center, deep gone into the dark. He legs the bases and crosses home with his head down, then strolls back behind the backstop and leans into his long-lost conversation as if nothing had just happened.

An old Yiddish proverb says, Gold will never rust. Goldy glows.

◆

Gerig Park in Ocala: high crumbling concrete walls surrounded the whole place, and the old covered grandstand behind homeplate leaned as if it might crash to the ground at any moment. (It since has.)

The Indianapolis Clowns were putting us through a rapid-fire batting practice, with a pitcher throwing hard off the mound. One bad swing and you're out — the only way to stay at the plate is to keep getting base hits.

Rob Marto is up there for twenty minutes, spraying line drives all over the field and tobacco juice all over homeplate. He finally wears that pitcher out, and they sign him up. One hard-hitting Clown.

◆

Memorial Field was the former home of the Oyster Bay Bombers Negro League team, and we adopted it as our home, along with the Bombers' name and legacy. The Bomber revivalists came in all colors, but we all wore black.

Shaggy at the edges, Memorial Field shimmered with the heat and humidity of Long Island north-shore summertimes. We drew crowds, though not quite like the original Bombers had. Two of our scrubs worked at the hotdog stand down the block, so postgame dogs and drinks were on the house.

It was said that our old coach Paulie had many children by many women, all over town. Paulie could never remember any of our names, so he called us all Lou. We wondered whether he called them Lou, too.

◆

Knights Field in Laurel, out on the North Fork, was constructed by the Mattituck Knights and assorted family and friends on the edge of a huge potato field. The Long Island Lighting Company donated lightpoles and erected them. They're a bit too low and a bit too bright, throwing harsh, blotchy yellow light on the rocky skin infield. It's a tough place to hit at night, with Rob Marto on the hill; you only see the top of his low fastball as it's blue bayou.

The infield is famous for its pebbles—just thousands of them, coin-sized. Thanks to them, all groundballs are adventures. I broke a finger on my throwing hand when a grounder took a last-hop left turn on me, bypassing my glove and getting my top hand good. Foul balls sail off into the black fields and we have to feel around for them in the dark among straight but snaky rows of potato plants. Late in the season is tough, for all the potatoes. We carry armloads home in exchange for lost game balls.

♦

McCloskey Field at Kenyon had the best-looking bad infield in the world. We called it McHopskey. It was all turf with cutouts for the bases, just like they do with Astroturf. But it was never properly rolled, so grounders never rolled properly. McHopskey coughed them up into your face like Bouncing Bettys.

In my first season with the Lords, a strange fungus took hold in the outfield, turning it a wretched brown. Whole sections peeled up like dead skin. One warm fall afternoon, termites hatched in the turf and flew up by the thousands to hover like a living battle-fog. You had to run with your mouth closed to keep from inhaling pestilence.

And then there was Warren G. Moore, who fell dead at second base. I wept for the old gamer in the dugout after all the others had gone.

♦

Mount Vernon Nazarene College: a field so fine, not a single blade of grass is out of place. The tiny chips of infield brick dust seem individually hand-selected. It occupies the middle of campus like a cathedral in a small town square.

The Naz players are as drilled in the game's fundamentals as they are in this field's maintenance. Righteously. Their pitchers' pickoff throws always find the near corner of first base, right at ground level.

If these players pray upon this field (as surely they do) their prayers are answered in spades. They've made real baseball heaven here.

♦

Doubleday Field in Cooperstown: we sit through a tortured weekend of rain before getting in a single game on Sunday afternoon. Sprinting onto that field is like seeing yourself in the Movietone News, shaking hands with Kenesaw Mountain Landis and tipping your cap to Wendell Willkie. The dugouts inset into the brick backstop walls are the tiniest anywhere — there's barely room on the bench for nine men, cheek to cheek. With the Babe in attendance, it had to be standing room only, and not just for the fans. Everyone grabs a pocketful of infield dirt as a keepsake.

Young Bulls

If not for ballgames, I'd never have known Fred Schwartz. We met on a diamond and I wound up playing modified fast-pitch softball with his Smithtown Bulls for a couple seasons, then later MSBL baseball. Fred has had a marvelous amateur ballplaying career by virtue of his own game (still going at 52), a strong hand in his sons' development (until they got too good for him on a ballfield) and focused, intelligent effort expended on behalf of all the young players he's coached. We've become friends of the sort who converse with years-long gaps in-between, but Fred's a constant — an eternal kid of the best sort. I'll know him all my life, if I'm lucky.

He grew up at the very edge of NYC in Bellrose, Queens— the same neighborhood that produced Goldy, but Fred was a few years older. They played Little League and sandlot games at a glorious ballpark wedged into the middle of this large garden apartment complex, a place called Glen Oaks. The Glen Oaks Oval occupied the center of a big traffic circle in the middle of the complex, and was all chain-link heaven — the literal and spiritual center of the neighborhood. Tall fences contained it, but could barely encompass the dreaming swarms of players, all the "nonhoodlums and aspiring jocks" of this crowded working-class margin of NYC. It was a proving ground, with the proof in the playing. The baseball kids weren't better than the hoodlums, they just occupied their time differently — and made themselves better in the process, at baseball first. Fred lived in a house just outside the apartment complex, but everybody was welcome at the Oval.

Oval baseball can only be described as essential. The ages ranged from little kids to big boys to young men, with adult coaches in attendance if not always in control. As at any baseball occasion there were stars and there were others. Downtown Kenny Brown was a star, as was Goldy when he grew a little; Fred was a small kid, and a solid eager player, the perennial sure-handed shortstop. Not a star, exactly, he was one of the yeoman others who carried the game in the sense that you have to put nine out there; like Jimmy Fogarty said, someone's got to play first base, and somebody's gotta play short, and someone's gotta pitch. But these yeomen don't see it that way — they see themselves at the very center of all action, and they carry the narrative. Heroes make themselves evident so the others can watch and aspire, suffering in being the opposition or celebrating as teammates. Legend carries their names forth, but in the end, it's just Oval baseball, and the yeomen come away with their rightful share. As anywhere else short of the bigs, it's the fundament — the essence. Players — stars and others — carry the game forward with all the ownership they have in its occasion, knowing best what comes from themselves.

Fred's a judge on Long Island now with his own law practice and two sons just out of college. Both boys played Division-I baseball, and his first son Michael was good enough to warrant a look. Fred and the other coaching dads worked hard at what they did, putting every spare bit of parental energy into fostering the game in their kids. Some of the dads ultimately came back to playing ball themselves to answer their high-school wisecrackers' challenges. They entwined themselves in ballplaying alongside their kids until the kids got so good the dads could no longer compete — couldn't hit their fastballs, didn't want to get in front of their screaming grounders. The father-son handoff is clean in that context; fathers can watch their sons move beyond them with sure satisfaction. And the aging Smithtown Bulls maintained their own pace and carried their own game onward. Eventually Fred would walk on with MSBL teams from Atlanta and elsewhere to play in national tournaments, and acquit himself well. As starting stranger with the Philadelphia Phifties last year he did battle against the national over–50s in Phoenix, competing against "young guys" of only 50 or 51. Age is the leveler, always; few elders can truly play the whole game with younger guns. But you play within your age bracket and you find you can compete, because as Fred says, the limits of your arm are matched by the other guy's legs. The game comes back to childhood in that way, when no one can do it all but everyone can do it at a certain speed for a certain distance. Over-thirty, over-forty, and over-fifty are all stakes in the ground that keep competition real.

How wonderful then, in that cyclic way, it was the kids who drew the dads back into the game. Kids are a strange bunch; their sheer diversity can be outrageous, even in one small town or large garden apartment complex. Sorted by age, the 10-to-12-year-olds comprise a range of little boyhood and growth spurts, and the 13-to-15-year-olds (like my Market Dogs) show a next-level mix of pre- and full-bore puberty. Some go through it late. Fred coached one kid who didn't hit puberty until he was 18 — a small, squeaky kid and a terrific ballplayer. Fred protected this kid against other coaches' counsel to cut him — "he's too little," was the common wisdom. Fred, being small of stature himself, heard none of it. At 5-foot-3 and 118 pounds, Jimmy Goelz barely made his high school team, getting a total of four at-bats in his four-year career. But now he's at Dodgertown in Vero Beach, playing professional baseball — a second baseman (god bless him), he hit .282 last year for the Yakima Bears of the Short-Season A Northwest League. Drafted in the 16th round out of college, he's a little guy who made it because another little guy saw something that was not to be denied in either of them.

Jim Goelz knew how good he could be, even in his 12-year-old body. His dad was a great softball player, and had been a Yankee batboy in the early 1970s, so there was a thin genetic link to the Show. Jim's father kindled it like a life-saving flame in wintry woods. He passed on everything he'd learned from Yankee second-baseman Horace Clarke to his little son, and the kid listened with his whole self, and saw it through 'til his body finally grew. Fred now says, "I wish for him what he wishes for himself. You get to coach these kids and make an impact on their lives, and you realize there's so much to this. It goes beyond making it to the Show, and it goes beyond the bucks and all these other issues — it's making a mark, being the best player you can possibly be in your own time. You take it as far as you can, and maybe get your education, and maybe more. And if you're lucky and talented enough, when you're forty everyone wants to sit and talk with you about the time you spent in the minor leagues riding those buses." It's all about laying down a pattern of work and success. Baseball delivers on that.

♦

The elder Smithtown Bulls played in the Long Island Modified Softball Association for a number of years, then over–30 hardball in the MSBL. They did it to show their kids how to play the game, and to show themselves how to improve their play even while battling the limits of aging. Their best player was Frank Catalanotto, a Smithtown softball legend in his own time. Catalanotto Senior was getting flack from Junior, and to prove he could still play, he played. It spurred the kid along, giving father and son a place of refuge from whatever else they chose to disagree upon, as well as a clear path for the kid to surpass the father. Frank Jr. is on the Texas Rangers now, in the bigs. And the running rant from the dads is, if you just hit as good as your father, you'd have been in the bigs two years sooner! A tenth-round pick in 1992, Frank Jr. was drafted as a second basemen (god bless him, too) and made it past all the shortstops to the Show. He's now in his third season, battling for the starting job. Like all good second basemen, he owns that bag. In 286 at-bats last year, he hit .276 with a bunch of doubles.

♦

At 16 or so young guys become powerful, and if they stay true and love the work they can enter another realm of play, taking the first big step up the competitive pyramid with high-school and college ball. If they break through and surface at this level they can begin to really learn their athletics and know how to shine from the inside out.

Fred's son Mike was like that. He rose and shone. In high school, Mike was recruited by Fairfield University in Connecticut, a MAAC conference Division-I school. He was a lefty-hitting catcher and third baseman, a three-year starter at Fairfield. He majored in economics and graduated from a five-year program in four. Fred marvels at what Mike did, and all such kids — all the schoolwork along with the 50-plus hours each week at practice and games. College baseball is long days of travel and game, doubled up with long nights on the books. It demands real time management and serves as a proving ground for handling life's challenges in multiples.

When mononucleosis hit Mike in his senior year at Fairfield, it ended his college baseball career in an instant, plowing him over like a blindside truck as the reality of it sunk in. Fred tells the story — he was there when the diagnosis was delivered and Mike was transported out of his game:

"Mike was flagging — I could see it. He hit a ball in the gap, and normally would've been standing on third, but he glided into second and stopped. That was not Mike, not at all. He was tired and sore, just not feeling right, but he wanted to play through it. You know. You deny the pain. So we took him in for tests, and we're there in the doctor's office for the results, and the doc tells Mike he can't play ball. And Mike says, like, today? You mean I can't play today? And the doc says No, I mean you can't play the rest of this season. We're going to have to shut you down. Mike's in disbelief, shaking his head. So I'm a little tired! he says, I'll just rest more. Oh, you'll rest more is right, says the doc. So I'll play anyway? No, says doc. But what's the big deal, says Mike. What if you get hit in the spleen? What if a ball hits you there? Yeah, what if, Mike says. I can protect my spleen! And he laughs. No you can't, says the doc. You could easily get hit there. And so what if I did, the kid asks. The doctor replies, You could die, Mike."

"Oh."

◆

The value of playing college ball, doubling the disciplines of scholarship and athletics, is finally a more useful and achievable goal for most than thinking pro. You don't have to get to the pros to have a great career and to make your mark. Learning to manage time, to achieve on several fronts even though time is squeezed — your sport, plus academics, plus everything else you have to do — makes capable men and women. And how many people can say they played on a Division-I level? Or even D-III? Not many. The pyramid narrows sharply, and climbing it — taking even those first few steps — brings you quickly into rarified air. You begin to see up-close just how steep the climb is, and just how hard life's pyramids can be, and just how proud the effort. It's the pattern of work and success that gives it all back — in baseball and other sports, too.

Mike's now working his way into a business career, with focus and certain goals. There's no tragedy in either of Fred's sons for leaving the game after some college ball. Both of them use the experience now without even knowing it.

And the Bulls remain on the long run toward home. Fred's pal Richie Collins, a CPA, is 56 years young and still a trooper second baseman. He's possessed of fantasy-camp crazy love, playing each year with the sixties and seventies Mets at Port St. Lucie. John Miller, another Bull, didn't play high-school ball but became a track star in college; his son Benjy went to Liberty University, was an all-conference pitcher, and was drafted by the San Francisco Giants. Robin Czemba was (and is) the consummate Bull pitcher who even at age 49 runs the ball past everyone. George Kuehnel, drafted young and then hurt, came back to play and is now 52, playing all these years. Hunter Brett was another late-day great for the Bulls. And on and on.

◆

It comes to an end for everybody ... "except for meshuggenahs like you and me," Fred says on the phone. Like crazy men, we laugh.

8

FIELDWORK

First Base

It's the most common coaching mistake made at all amateur levels—from casual softball to competitive baseball. Take the guy who can't do anything else defensively—can't throw, can't move, doesn't catch very well—and stick him at first base. The assumption is that it's the easiest position to play. My take is that its the easiest position to screw up, and the premier place to cost your infield outs and your team wins.

In 1966, when the Yanks had suddenly sunk to the very bottom after years at the very top, when everybody got old at the same time and a succession of "next Mickey Mantles" (Tom Tresh, at that point) were failing to pan out, the Yankee brass moved The Mick to first base to extend his career. He had come up to the bigs as a shortstop, and was a stellar centerfielder, but his take on playing first was that "it was the hardest thing I ever tried to do in baseball." His knees were shot and the rest of his body was held together by athletic tape, but that wasn't his excuse. It's a tough position to play well, especially for a right-hander. Positioning your feet, keeping soft hands—letting the ball come to you—those throws in the dirt, a runner pounding toward you as you wait for an infielder to get off a veering throw across the diamond—guys who do it well keep runners off the bases, helping fellow infielders by taking imperfect throws and finessing them into quick outs. Bad first basemen cross up their feet, recoil at short hops, and sometimes drop

Fogarty ejecting, George waiting for some heat, 1998.

solid throws that hit them in the mitt. They keep the infield unsettled and no lead safe.

Watching a great first baseman like Keith Hernandez is an object lesson in readiness and presence of mind, and the importance of that position. In those few great Mets years of the mid–1980s, Hernandez redefined what a first baseman could bring to baseball defense. He captained the infield from first, and his decisive moves made that right infield side a trap for hitters and baserunners alike. In bunting situations with a runner at first, he'd work an "up and back" more deftly, with better timing, than anyone had ever seen. He'd hold the runner, then break in suddenly to charge the batter, fielding the bunt (if the batter got one down) and firing to second to get the lead out. And as soon as runners got comfortable with taking a big secondary lead after he charged, he'd fake a charge then leap back to the bag for a pickoff throw, stopping many a runner in his tracks for an easy and embarrassing out. A variant of this play involved faking the charge then faking the retreat, getting the runner diving back while the pitcher threw to the plate. He kept those runners on tenterhooks, even when his pitcher didn't have a great move to first. And by jumping into batters' fields of vision, he provided effective distraction and cut down on their swings if they were swinging away. He had sure hands and a strong firstbase arm; but most of all, he had a plan, and the ability to communicate subtly with his pitcher, catcher and infielders so that everyone knew what was up. His intuitive stopwatch was well calibrated, with an intensity of focus that set the tone for that working-man's infield. You could see it in his eyes, reading the action around him — constant and quick.

Not all first basemen work the "up and back" so surely. This was borne out early in the 1998 season in a Pirate defeat of the Mets at Shea Stadium in my birthplace of Flushing, New York.

From a news account: "The controversial play occurred with Pittsburgh leading 2-0 and catcher Keith Osik [out of Shoreham-Wading River High School] at firstbase with none out and pitcher Francisco Cordova at bat. The Mets tried to pick off Osik with what Valentine called an 'up-and-back' play. First baseman John Olerud took a few steps toward home as if to field a bunt, faking the runner, then ran back toward the base to accept a pickoff throw.

"The throw was not quite in time. First-base umpire Bruce Dreckman merely signaled Osik safe, but [home-plate umpire Frank] Pulli called a balk, moving Osik to second. That led to a debate between Pulli and Valentine that continued for nearly five minutes as they pointed fingers in one another's faces and pursued each other around the diamond.

"Pulli made a judgment call. The rule indicates a balk call if a first baseman is not moving toward the base when the throw comes from the pitcher. Pulli said Olerud was not — a notion supported by Olerud, who said the timing between him and [Mets' pitcher Bobby] Jones was off. 'He was a little bit early on that throw, and I was still moving forward a little bit,' Olerud said. Said Pulli: 'The rule states that the first baseman goes up the line, and the pitcher throws him the ball from the pitcher's mound, and in the umpire's judgment, he doesn't think the first baseman is making a play on the runner, it's a balk. It's plain and simple, end of story.'

"Valentine said every team has a similar play in its bunt-defense repertoire. 'This isn't something I pulled out of some Little League playbook.'"

♦

The real dilemma with first base is, since even at the pro level the defensive requirements are underrated, coaches want a hitter there. They'll take light bats up the middle, but they definitely want some pop at the corners. This makes some sense; the catcher, middle infielders and centerfielder are the spine of your defense, and if you don't have strong defense up the middle, you're screwed. But at the same time you've got to get an enormous amount of run production from first in order to justify putting a klutz there. The guy's got to be a constant run-producing machine to make up for the lost outs.

On balance, I favor a strong glove at first, and I'll take outs over runs. I think strong defense tips that balance and wins more ballgames. Hitting comes and goes; defense is there for 27 outs every game. And, flipping that coin, bad defense can hurt too much, too constantly, for your hitters or your pitchers to keep up. Especially with a steel mitt and feet of clay at first.

Courage Is a Catcher

A catcher sets up behind the dish with the diamond vectoring out before him. The point of the plate aims right at his cup; he has the entire field in his face — foul line to foul line out to the fences, and closer in, the mound and infield, and to either side, the dugouts. Breathing down his neck is the homeplate ump, the master of ceremonies for every pitch to follow. An ump sometimes rests his hand on the catcher's shoulder as a pitch comes in, dancing out of the way should a passed ball skip on by. They're closer than any other two guys on the field, until players and plays collide. No matter what happens, these two resume their positions just behind the plate for whatever's next. Their readiness paces the game as nothing else can.

A catcher sometimes struggles to keep his pitcher on his pace. He sets himself up and gets ready to flash signs, but has to wait for lefty, who may be wiping his brow out there on the mound, or staring off into space. The catcher coaxes his pitcher to get it on, get it moving, keep it low. Gimme it here, is what his body language says. Hit me with a hard one. Make my mitt-hand hurt.

A catcher better be paying attention, and better not slow lefty down if he's trying to work fast — not even when pain intrudes. The catcher's in tune with all of his infield, and he sees how the pace is working them. He also feels the swing of the bat as the hitter pumps himself ready. He's right there at the crux of the game.

The pitcher may own the strike zone on a given day, but the catcher guards it. He coaxes pitches through it, around the hitter's wheelhouse or into the dirt if the guy seems anxious to take a hack. His body blocks the short hops and uncurls in a flash for the high fastball heading for the wild blue yonder. Whatever else happens, he settles in for the next one, gesturing gently to calm lefty down, tapping his chest pad to put a play on for his infield. The game is all his to receive. He gives to get.

More managers are former catchers than anything else, not for no reason. For years, the saying has been "if you want to get to the bigs, catch." That bears unpacking.

A talented player at any position can get to the bigs if he's good enough, and lucky; but a guy who might not make it as an outfielder or infielder might make it as a catcher, if he's a very good catcher and he can hit some. It's a bit like lefty pitchers; good ones are in short supply, and marginally-good ones sometimes make it, and sometimes find ways to thrive. Catchers who are more than marginal are treasures; catching is tough, awfully tough, and most managers will give up some offense for a catcher who can handle the plate, lend pitchers confidence, and find ways to win. If a guy can do all that and also pack a wallop with his bat, he's golden. Someone once said, "Yogi, you're ugly," and Yogi answered: "So? I don't hit with my face."

In the amateur trenches, good catchers are doubly golden. I've played with some remarkable ones — Wilbur was one such, for the Bombers. Quick, sure-handed and very smart, Wilbur at his best was a force, a unifying intelligence behind the plate. He'd cajole umpires with a smile but never give ground to a runner, using keen balance and his left elbow to deal damage when he had to. And he could hit, especially in the clutch. In the long run, Wilbur was much better to play with than against. On the bench he was a baseball Buddha.

◆

My two most memorable catchers, for sheer courage and grace, were Scott Anders of the Angels and Cardinal Bob Margolin. Their stories are worth relating.

Scott is a big man — 6'2", about 220 pounds. He has the classic catcher build — broad, muscular and thick — like the proverbial brick shithouse, but with a keen athletic poise and a boyish bounce. He has keen eyes and a ready smile, but watching him work behind the plate you see something else; behind the mask he's all business— smooth and efficient, quick to flip the ball back to the pitcher, steadfast in his crouch. He doesn't waste time, he uses it; his right hand taps his mask as if to say to his pitcher, "Here I am; throw to me." He stays in the crouch so the pitcher can work as quickly as possible, and his infielders love him for that.

Now nearing forty, Scott still plays in a college summer league in central Ohio, often driving fifty miles or more to get to a game. In the winter he referees high school football and basketball games, as much to stay in baseball shape as for the extra income. He's married with three daughters, so he has loyal fans at every game.

Scott's career is telling. He was a baseball standout at Ohio Dominican College, and was drafted by the Chicago Cubs in 1985. He caught for two seasons at the A-level minors with the Geneva Cubs and then the Peoria Cubs. In Geneva, in the second game of his pro career, he was beaned by a fastball that shattered his nose and his left optic lobe, and detached his left retina. Scott missed most of that season, but stayed in Geneva doing chores for the team (carrying water, as they say) and got back in there for the last twenty games and the playoffs. The next year they sent him to Peoria, a step up the A-ball ladder. He was starting catcher there until July, when the Cubs drafted hometowner Joe Girardi and club management decided that he should play in Peoria. Scott still got innings, but the next spring the Cubs decided to give Girardi more playing time in Peoria (Girardi eventually made it to the bigs with the Cubs, and has since had the great good fortune to win three World Series rings with the New York Yankees). When they told Scott they were sending him back to Geneva, he refused the assignment. He went home to Zanesville, and because he was still legally under contract to the Cubs, he couldn't even play amateur ball. The Cubs invited him to spring training in 1987, but he didn't go—married now and with a child, he got halfway to the airport and turned around. The Cubs had paid him $700 a month his first year and $850 the next; he did not feel in his heart he could ask his family to shoulder such sacrifice now, so he sacrificed his dream instead.

Taking his pay and packing it in was one of the toughest decisions he ever had to make; Scott had invested everything into his march toward the majors. But he could not abide with the demotion; in pro ball, you're either moving up or moving out. His ghastly injury had cost him precious time, and the situation was, on some levels, political; as is always the case in the pro minors, your skill must be matched with luck and good timing. Girardi was a Peoria boy, and had been both a standout player and a brilliant student at Northwestern. He already had an agent, which was rare for minor leaguers in the 1980s, and with all of his natural Illinois connections he was the new fair-haired boy at Peoria and, soon, Chicago. As happens often to many, Scott was eclipsed and written off as damaged goods in the span of a season and a half. It's a rare player who recovers quickly from a bad beaning without losing his aggressive edge as a hitter; conventional baseball wisdom dictates that such a player will never be what he once was or might have been.

So Scott gave up the dream but not the ghost. He returned home to Zanesville, Ohio, where his voluntary retirement kept him under control of the Cubs until 1990, when he sought and got his release. Once released, he began playing amateur ball with the Senior Pioneers, suddenly the big shark in a much smaller pond. Mark Davis heard of him and tracked him down, convincing him to come play for the MSBL Columbus Angels. The first time he walked on the field to catch for us was in Marion, Ohio, for a game against the Marion Marlins. Scott hit two home runs that day, barely missing a third off the high right field fence. His catching was a big step up from what we'd had before. Our pitchers loved throwing to him for his skill at framing pitches, the speed with which he worked, his pitch calling and the confidence he exuded and shared. Scott saw things in the game that none of us had ever glimpsed, and we began to raise our game to approximate his. From second base I could get his attention with a wink or the flick of a finger. His calm steadiness behind the plate would put baserunners to sleep, then as quick as a rifle shot he would pick someone off second base. We middle infielders had to be on our toes to avoid being picked off ourselves by his bullet throws. He brought our entire infield up a big notch.

That he would leave Peoria but not the game is a testament to Scott's devotion. His battered face never stopped wanting to be there, and as an amateur player, he brought precious game sense and a generous serving of his graying boyish delight to the occasion. On the bench, he could be coaxed into telling stories from the Peoria days, and had no problem in doing so. But he wasn't there for that. He came to play, to elevate the game to a better level, and to coax courage from everyone around him simply by doing what he did with a consummate sense of belief.

♦

Believers are often unaware of their own courage. With an outward focus, inner grace manifests without self-reflection, absent the self-consciousness that causes others to falter. Time may come later to dwell in memory and grit the teeth with pain's echo, but the present is consumed with getting things done, with pure play — the selfless expression of grace under pressure. Such was the character of Bob Margolin's game, too. It ate him alive and fed him its bounty.

Bob is a county attorney, a big bear of a man with a full mustache. His broad face is usually occupied by a warm smile or a rueful grin. Pain finds its way there too, inevitably, but it never wins out. In the rare moments when the pain shows, Bob is quick to mask it. I've watched him literally shake it off like a grizzly shaking off snow in a blizzard.

As his teammate, I once caused him pain on the Cardinal bench after he hurled a pickoff throw into left field, allowing a runner to trot home from third. I was mad at myself and the whole team — we were playing flat-footed, half-assed — and when I said "Let's just hand them some runs" he took it to mean him, understandably, and he blanched. I regretted it as soon as I said it, but there it was — spoken in anger, shamefully. Bob just got up and limped away.

That he forgave me before the inning ended was characteristic. A true athlete, Bob played with a progressive disease that was slowly taking away his control of his legs. He always limped, and when he ran his big upper body fought with his lower half to keep moving and stay on his feet. When catching, he moved slowly and heavily around homeplate, sometimes standing on one leg to try to regain strength. But he was a fine catcher, with the softest hands you ever saw. In his crouch he was balanced, skilled at framing pitches and digging them out of the dirt. But he had a tough time coming out of the crouch. When he lost his balance he usually held the ball, but sometimes hurled it, and sometimes got his man. Blocking the plate, he was immovable — I never once saw him flinch at a coming hit. He'd sprawl on his back and blow dirt from his mouth, showing mitt and ball to the ump for the out. Pain was the interest on his loan, and he made all his payments right on time.

Mine is long overdue, but here it is, Bob. All true.

Fitzy & Fatty

As a player of long standing I've had all sorts of coaches. They've run the gamut from the blessedly gifted to the very worst possible — from Ronnie Fitz in the sandlots teaching baseball and courage by example, to a guy who hated himself and baseball deep in his soft belly and did his urgent best to make his players hate the game more. That's what you get, if you play long enough: the whole wide range of coaching skill and lack thereof, all guided by its own bright light or dull sense and brought to bear upon players in the game's occasion.

The best thing about Ronnie Fitz was his ability to both spread the game like gospel and demonstrate its miracles like Jesus himself. The strength of his own belief gave him this surpassing grace. He communicated it by design in his posture, in his gait, and in fluid muscular expression which he bore effortlessly, even as he grimaced with back pain or took a hard hit at second base, or threw down his mitt to fight. His ego was as big as the game (in the game) and made its mark on us there; elsewhere he was quiet, confident, slyly mischievous but kind. On a ballfield he was magnetic, drawing us in like iron filings, creating a field of energy with an inexpressible rightness all about it. A master of details, he always took time to correct our mistakes and to make sure we recognized his own, which he signaled with a deep breath of determination to get it right next time. By playing with unbounded joy within the bounds of a higher calling he modeled the best moves, the best attitude, and a winning mix of passion and skill, guts and smarts. Years later, as Gorillas, we called it heads and hands. But it was really all about soul. For me, Ronnie Fitz will always be the heart of baseball incarnate, rising from the bulldozed valley of State with the clarity of a Zen gong, the mastery of a monk, his sheer lightness of being resembling nothing less than a nimble monkey in its favorite tree.

What wins out in the end is this love. Learned and earned in motion, it is the ultimate keeper — more than any treasured memento, worth saving and savoring. It was his gift to give, and he gave it all.

Fitzy's golden coaching coin had a flip side that me took three long lucky decades to encounter. As was my good fortune, after Fitzy came a succession of Little League, varsity and amateur coaches who all knew something, and who all had something of value to give. But then came Fatty.

On the field, he was never sure of what to do next; in practices, he worked from a checklist to keep his bearings, but was never able to measure a pace to bring out the best in players, and so managed to reinforce the worst play while letting rare moments of success pass by unnoticed, unremarked and unrewarded. In games, his instincts undercut any movement toward success, interrupting momentum and spotlighting physical embarrassment at every opportunity. The embarrassment was his own, but he choreographed it through his players, and liked to bark at it. A poor sport through and through, he wore his lack of soul on his sleeve and was widely disliked and rightfully distrusted.

Leadership talent can motivate and inspire good play from either side of affection; coaches can be loved or hated and still be effective. With the soul of a vengeful bureaucrat, Fatty ruled in confusion with mixed signals, always out of synch. If ever there was a more anxious loser, I pray never to encounter him anywhere near a ballfield.

As for Ronnie Fitz — I'd sprint behind him into a gun battle armed with a slingshot — anytime, anywhere. And we'd find a way to win it.

Fogarty's Wake

reader taking the plunge (so to speak, so to read) into *Finnegans Wake* finds first words leading (but not beginning, since it's already begun) a long torrent of recurring dreamflow —

> riverrun, past Eve and Adam's, from swerve of shore to bend
> of bay, brings us by a commodious vicus of recirculation

— in perhaps the most articulate actualizing of dream we have in the language. James Joyce begins Finnegan mid-sentence, and ends it likewise —

> Given! A way a lone a last a loved a long the

— and by that last definite article circles ("the") reader from the last line back to the book's beginning to pick up its first phrase. Completely circular, the book finds physical dreaming at the level of water and song-birds, but in a man, with words and pure sound. Finnegan the father dreams of his family, his sons most vividly, those selves as realizations of his dreaming as he begot them. What Joseph Campbell calls "body wisdom" sings in the wake of this dreaming, locating a collective order that has all to do with a river running, with water falling from cloud and returning to cloud in mythical cycles. "Round and round and round and round" as Campbell wrote of Finnegan "is the flow of the river of time. The coming into being of the world and its going out of being." In this "eternal return," "nothing happens that has not happened a million times before" while each moment is, in itself, a "final term." The wake neither begins nor ends, really. Time runs through it like a perplexed pitcher running poles, back and forth, breathing deep and daydreaming past words.

It's useful, here, for Joseph Campbell to filter the story as he knows it: "There is an Irish-American vaudeville song called 'Finnegan's Wake,' and it is a story of an Irish hod carrier. I don't know whether anyone knows anymore what a hod carrier was. Before buildings were made of metal with wonderful mechanical elevators going up and down, they were made of bricks. When a building was being built, the bricks had to be carried up, and so men went up scaffolds and ladders using a hod, this pole with a carrier at the top, to carry the bricks. They would go up with a load of bricks and come down with an empty hod: they were circulating matter and the spirit: carrying matter up to heaven and bringing spiritus ('air') back to earth. Here we have the cycle again, this wonderful cycle.

"So, one of these hod carriers was named Tim Finnegan, and his favorite pastime, like that of many Irishmen, was drinking Irish whiskey. The word whiskey is a Celtic word that means 'the spirit of life,' what activates the spirit in what we call 'spirits.' Jameson's Whiskey is made in Dublin from the water of the river Liffey, so it is (you might say) the delicious extract, the radiance ... and a radiance makes you drunk. So, full of radiance, full of the spirit that induces ecstasy and rapture, Tim Finnegan one day tumbles from the top of his ladder and falls down... His friends find him at the bottom of the ladder and take him home to have his wake. In the midst of this wake, someone is flinging around a bottle of whiskey, and it pours over Finnegan's body, and he jumps up and tries to join the dance at his own wake. Now if that were to happen — if the dreamer were to wake, if the sinner were to stop sinning — it would, of course, end the party. Since Joyce uses Finnegan as the man representing the Fall: the whole world is based on his remaining asleep. So the anxious mourners press down on him and say, 'Stay there! You just stay where you are.' And they reassure him that all is being taken care of in his absence."

♦

Young Michael Fogarty pitched for the nascent Stony Brook Cardinals in the early 1980s, prior to their entry into the fledgling MSBL. Mike literally pitched himself to death one afternoon after the ultimate rough outing. His wake was memorable.

The early pre–Cardinal games of Fogarty's day were of the pickup variety. There was a sufficient number of players to divide into two teams, but the teams would re-mix somewhat each week, with two captains choosing sides amidst the angling and wrangling of game politics. Some of the players were over thirty years old, some were in their twenties and a few were young kids. Two of the regular pitchers were youngsters, including 15-year-old Mark Napoli, the future Indianapolis Clown. He'd pitch for whatever side chose him, throwing good hittable fastballs at the older sluggers and striking them out with hard sliders.

Michael Fogarty also pitched. He'd seen himself as a pitcher ever since he was a kid, but he'd been a sickly kid, and the Scarlet Fever that engulfed him as a youngster had left him with heart damage. In his late twenties, he seemed physically older — prone to quick fatigue and a florid complexion. His doctor advised him in no uncertain terms to avoid overexertion, especially in hot weather. But Mike was a wobbly gamer, giving everything in whatever heat, fuck all. He'd sometimes get flushed and have to take an inning off and try to recover in a hot dugout. Mike's vision was poor, but he could run fast despite his scarred heart. He was an able athlete, as far as his body could take him, but his soul took him a bit further. He was all foreshortened effort with a bit of guile, and guile only takes you so far in this game. Mike got used to getting hit hard. He gave back in kind, heaving wild fastballs as hard as he could and nailing batters. Digging your own grave, is what pitching coaches call it. You try to throw harder and harder, and you wind up with runners on base, not winding up but pitching from the stretch, trying to hurl the ball beyond your ability, beyond reality, beyond life itself. In so doing you lose home plate and the strikezone grail.

It was a sweltering day at Ward Melville Field in Stony Brook, no shade anywhere, and most of the guys had downshifted a notch late in this long, hot, meandering game. Mike was on the mound in relief, the last available pitcher for his team, and he was working hard but having more than his usual control problems. He gave up some hits and runs, squandering a six-run lead, then loaded the bases on walks and hit batsmen. His face brilliant red and his shoulders heaving, he tried to coax a strike past a wily hitter and grooved it. The loud pong of ball on bat-head struck like a church bell, and Michael Fogarty watched the ball sail out of the park for a game-losing grand-slam home run. Staggering backwards off the mound, he whirled as if trying to see through fog, his crushed red face breaking through every teammate in the heavy humidity of sudden loss. He experienced the existential kick in the gut that resonates in failed effort — everything given, but not good enough. The heat of hellacious loss fields no excuse, offers no shade. Michael Fogarty wandered back to his car in a daze and drove slowly home.

Though he gave himself a day off to recover, Mike couldn't shake the searing flash of that loss, and after work on Tuesday he drove down to the schoolyard to throw against the wall. He threw long and hard, whipping the ball with a vengeance against the brick schoolhouse. Then he stopped, out of breath, and walked slowly back to his car. That's where the cops found him later that evening — slumped dead behind the wheel, his mitt still on his left hand, the ball still in it.

♦

Mike's uncle Jimmy Fogarty was another of the same clan of base-ball players dating back to New York harbor. That the two of them — athletic uncle and frail nephew — would show up together to play on Sunday afternoons was only natural; they came from solid Bushville lineage. Jimmy was born in 1938 in Brooklyn to a second-generation Irish father — who was a policeman out on Long Island — and a Ger-man-American mother who kept house. As a young, self-described "wiseguy lefty" Jimmy pitched for James Madison High in scholastic baseball tournaments, including one at Ebbets Field. He later had a walkon tryout there with the Brooklyn Dodgers as one of a bunch of young players trotted out to throw ten or fifteen pitches at big-league hitters. His beloved Dodgers treated him like they treated any bush kid, riding him hard. Pee Wee Reese and Duke Snider especially — "What the hell you doing out there you little shit? Just throw strikes like you're damn-well supposed to!" Fogarty's Irish temperament didn't take well to that, but he bit his tongue.

In those summers Jimmy Fogarty pitched for the Brooklyn Cadets, an amateur team, as well as for a team sponsored by Nathan's of Coney Island. They played against all sorts of amateur and semipro teams in the city and out on the Island. They faced young Sandy Koufax, at the time a hotshot Brooklyn lefthander playing under a basketball schol-arship at the University of Cincinnati and dropping in as a ringer for the Parkviews, a solid amateur Brooklyn baseball team. Koufax was wild and threw the ball impossibly hard; as Fogarty later said, you couldn't see the ball, but you could hear it. The Dodger scouts in atten-dance wondered how any amateur hitter could even foul one off against him, but Benny Galenti, a fierce little shortstop, slugged a double and a triple that day and the Cadets won, 2–1. Koufax was soon signed by the Dodgers for a lot of money and lured away from college; under the Bonus Baby rule of the time he was locked onto the major league ros-ter (the league offices thus discouraged teams from paying big money to young unproven players). He spent what should have been three minor-league years in the bush sitting instead on the Brooklyn bench, getting some innings and getting hammered — actually, they didn't hit him that much, but he walked a lot of them, and nailed a lot, too. You don't make yourself popular with your teammates when you hit batters without purpose. Retribution was inevitable, back then. But Koufax hung in there, and when the Dodgers moved to Los Angeles he found his command. In his last five big league seasons from 1962 through 1966 he was nearly unhittable, pitching 100 complete games and winning a World Series ring by sweeping the Yankees in 1963. Sandy went 111–34 over that four-year span with a quick, light-hitting but good-fielding team behind him. He quit after the '66 season, worried that repeated cortisone shots to his arthritic left shoulder were shortening his life. In that final season Sandy Koufax went 27–9 with a 1.74 ERA, then packed it in. To this day he remains an éminence grise, visiting Vero Beach each spring and counseling scores of young pitchers at Dodgertown, most possessing a bare fraction of his talent.

While Koufax matured in the bigs, Jimmy Fogarty labored in the Boston minors, hauling bricks so to speak under a short-term contract that paid him little. His father had lobbied him to accept a college scholarship; Jimmy chose to go pro for scant money and with little experience or protection. Then as now, certain players are guided and protected as investments, with organization money and scouting reputations riding on their shoulders; others are treated more like cannon fodder, run out there with little regard for their development and scant sympathy for their sore arms. Like a host of other aspiring pitchers, Jimmy got hurt on his way up the ladder, blowing his shoulder out and killing his chances for a big-league career. So it went, and so it goes. Money never comes without some measure of such corruption, and there are legions of former players who knocked on the door of big-league baseball and were orphaned by the politics of it all. Luck may be just the residue of design, but as the competitive levels get higher, luck is a winning hand. And it ain't a card game without others holding unlucky draws around the table.

Jimmy Fogarty quit the game and joined the Army, becoming a paratrooper and then playing Army ball against military teams and, occasionally, against convicts. Some of those prison teams were very good (as were the Army teams) — and why not, they had time to work on it. Besides, the convicts always played home games in front of boisterous, uniquely-loyal fans. Fogarty got into a dispute once with a very good prison player, going jaw to jaw with him, and when the umpire intervened this convict stepped back and said to both of them, "Don't you two fool around with me here cuz I'll kill you, right where you stand. I'm a lifer and there's nothing more they can do to me." Fogarty and the ump both backed off then and there, and the game continued towards its eventual parole.

Jimmy left the Army in 1961 and went to work for Otis Elevator, installing steel shafts in Manhattan's surging skyline. And twenty years later, when his wife saw Ken Robinson's ad in the newspaper — "bring a baseball with you Sunday morning — we'll choose sides and play ball!" — she showed it to Jimmy and urged him to go play. Fogarty showed up with his old mitt and picked up the game where he'd left it, right there in the grass, only now just for the joy of it.

Jimmy knew how to pitch with an old-timey windup, but his arm was shot. In ensuing years, when I played with him on the Cardinals, he struggled even in making cutoff throws from first to home. He was nonetheless a gamer and a sure moral force in the dugout, and he hit out of a keen low crouch, spraying line drives all over the field. He once rounded up all his relatives for a Sunday game of everyone vs. the Fogartys. Jimmy always said he enjoyed those early pickup games the most. There was no bullshit, only people playing ball for a good time.

As a fit role player and spiritual coach, Jimmy Fogarty embossed us with his stamp of game class. He knew what he could and couldn't do, all glorious memories aside, and he counseled George well, sometimes taking himself out late in a close game for a pinch runner. Suz once pinch-ran at his behest in a crucial inning; she stole third and scored on the overthrow, winning the game. The other team — a bunch of snarly kids — protested: this is a men's league! It doesn't say nothing about women! It didn't fly. Fogarty would have none of it from these whining punks. And by George's good graces, Suz was on the official roster.

That early Cardinal team had a host of bright and colorful regulars. A big lefty pitcher named Al Poxon started showing up; years before he'd made it to AA ball with Pittsburgh, but he never quite settled his mechanics, and so never quite got to the bigs. Al was a classic big lefty, goofy and grand with a great good nature, and Fogarty loved him. He out thought himself at every turn, making constant adjustments but never keeping a rhythm. At his best, he threw a mix of slow lefty stuff that baffled hitters; but when he was off just a little, he got hit hard. His Cardinal career ended when he got into an argument with his wife; she threw a big book at him, and Al put up his left arm to block it. Done.

Another Cardinal classic was Bob Powers. Bob was a right-handed pitcher who made small claims about having played in college. As we eventually found out, he had had a brilliant pitching career at St. John's University, going 30–5; it took some time to get that out of him. He showed up with an old dry mitt fished out of the back of the closet, telling George he hadn't pitched in ten years. But when he warmed up it was immediately evident that he was a real pitcher. George gave him the ball and Powers started the game for us, mowing down every batter he faced with hard, heavy, moving fastballs. Fogarty, on the sidelines, says to George, "No way this guy hasn't pitched in ten years! Look at him!" Bob took his no-hitter into the sixth with professional poise, fine control, and that hopping fastball. It was as if he'd fallen out of the sky into our lap — a clear winner, a force. One who didn't brag about where he'd been or bullshit about what he'd done. You had to ask him, and dig for details, and draw him out to get it all. Anyway, he's so good that old-pro Fogarty doesn't believe the ten-year claim. He isn't buying it for a minute. So here comes a sudden ripping linedrive right back at Powers, and in the instant he gets his glove up, but the ball goes right through the webbing and almost takes his ear off. Time is called and Powers strolls off the mound, giving the mitt a good long look and shaking his head with an ironical smile. It's ten years dry, its leather is crazed and cracked, and now it has a big hole where the web used to be. Fogarty looks at it and George says, "OK, so now you believe him?"

You can tell a lot about a guy by his mitt. In Bob Powers' case, you had to take that good long look. Jimmy Fogarty was the same way. There was a lot of the game under the crazed leather of his skin.

As good as Powers was, the very best pitcher in those Cardinal years was a guy named Bill Dotter. Another humble man of quiet-but-sure demeanor, Dotter threw the hardest of anyone George ever faced. He was the goods, almost unhittable at that level — as George said, "Just too good." Once after Dotter struck him out, George says to him, respectfully, "You're really throwing hard!" and Dotter replies, with equanimity, "Yeah, but you had really good swings"— as sincere as a human being can be. Dotter pitched for a couple more years, then came back to play one more game and broke his collarbone sliding into home. Done.

◆

At a normally-decorous funeral home in Babylon, New York, Michael Fogarty's teammates dressed him in his Cardinal uniform and hung his spikes from the coffin handle. They draped his mitt on his left hand and cradled a ball in his right. His grandfather provided a big floral wreath in the shape of a baseball — all white mums with red carnations as the stitches. His brother John brought along a big galvanized garbage can full of icewater and beer, with a bottle of whisky on the side. You had to drink — there was no refusing — and even the teetotalers got sloshed. John wore his shiny new black suit, and spent the afternoon plunging his arm deep into the icewater to get the next guy a cold one from the bottom. His sleeve was soaking wet all the way up to the shoulder, but John was philosophical. Michael died unmarried, with no son; baseball was his dream and first passion. The scene in the funeral home was draped with sentiment, a mix of laughter and mourning occasioned as much for the game as for its latest victim. The assembled aunts and uncles and cousins went along with it because it gave young Michael Fogarty's passing a focus. He died doing what he did at his best. He carried the long family campaign on his silent chest, right there at the letters.

◆

When I left the Cardinals Jimmy Fogarty was still playing; he's since retired, so they say. But with a Fogarty you never know. He could still get up to rejoin the dance if the crowd in his head roars

a way a lone a last a loved a long the

Off the Record

I think it must be hardest on those who have knocked on the door, and who might have made it through, but didn't. Some had real talent, and now look back with real regret in knowing this: if they knew then what they know now, they just might have made it through.

Had they been savvy instead of just gung-ho, had they seen how to play the politics of it, they might have had a chance to get somewhere in pro ball. They think of guys they knew, guys they played with and against, guys who made it — and they remember being just as good, then and there. Getting that hit or striking that guy out, feeling that confidence, the blessed arrogance based on nothing but an instant, based on dreams and the strength of young tissue. Time and tissue both break.

It's harder on those guys, and they're harder yet on themselves. They don't show up at local ballgames talking big talk about where they've been and what they've done; in their eyes, they did little, and could have done more. But they walk out onto the field and pick up a ball, and you can see it, what they must have had, then. Eternal regret comes of age. We could all be more than we knew we were, when.

◆

"I was a wiseguy growin' up in Brooklyn, a little stinkin' wiseguy, and I did have some talent, as a matter of fact I thought I was a pretty good pitcher. They were gonna give me some sort of baseball scholarship to go to college, and across the kitchen table my father advised me to take the scholarship, but I wanted to go play pro. So I go away, and I'm away, and now it's a money aspect, and I'm seventeen or eighteen years old, and everything's money. You play on a handshake, and I didn't realize it at the time — I didn't know one way or another what was goin' on, with contracts and what-not — who the hell knew? — I thought it was like playin' ball for fun. It was NOT that. So everybody says, they gotta have an investment in ya, you're goin' away and they're gonna use you like a piece of meat. Because I didn't realize that somebody has to go out and play shortstop, and somebody has to pitch and somebody has to catch, because you have to put nine people on the field. So now, when you have high-priced investments, you take care of those people, like business. And your eyes start to open up, even as a seventeen- or eighteen-year-old punk. So you start to see that a guy who had, at that time, a few thousand dollars invested in him is being protected — he's not starting and relieving and starting like you are. And all of a sudden your arm is hangin' and all of a sudden you don't have a fastball no more and you start throwin' curves and your elbow is killin' you, but you go out there because you're gettin' a menial sum. And the next thing you know you start feelin' sorry for yourself and you wind up in the local saloons with the beer cans. And your life is a complete failure! And that's how I felt about my life before I was twenty-one. I'm tellin' you, it's not glorious."

◆

Looking back can be difficult. Lots of people suffer that for all sorts of reasons— race or age or religion, or not being the fair-haired boy at the right moment, not catching the right guy's eye. Or just not being good enough. Failure sometimes happens when you're not looking, and only comes home to roost later, when it's too late to do anything about it. And whether you failed on your own merit or you failed because you were cheated in some way, it's still a matter of knocking on the door and not getting through — not having someone on the other side to hold it open for you. You see some big-time pro athletes, and you know that doors have been held open for them all along. Some make the most of that, and some squander it. With age comes this reckoning: what might have been. It's not necessarily glorious. But light does gather.

Goosechasers

I work now with an R&D group at AT&T Labs here in Ohio, developing large-scale network software. We're a group of about seventy from all over the world — Americans, Indians, Pakistanis, Chinese, Russians, Romanians, Koreans— a divers mix of souls, all focused on building logic machines and human interfaces on the monstrous AT&T Global Intelligent Network. We'd just moved into our new building in Reynoldsburg — where the company placed bricks engraved with our names in the courtyard — when we got a call from Lisa at TS Tech (a Honda subsidiary down the street) — asking, did we want to form a co-ed softball league and play on their new softball field?

Hoo-eee! Did we!

Company softball can span the gamut from hell-bent competitive to purely recreational. Our team was clearly of the latter sort, with players from abroad who'd never played the game in their lives, but were eager to learn this American pastime. We also had some real players — guys and women who had played competitive ball in school and in local leagues. It was a wonderful mix, and we approached the season with good humor but also with a desire to win, no matter how limited the depth of our talent. The truth was, our competition was no better — more uniformly American, perhaps, but nonetheless playing for fun with limited means.

Herewith is the e-mail trail of our season's highlights, beginning with our first victory after three getting-to-know-you losses.

♦

GOOSECHASERS ROMP, 16–6

REYNOLDSBURG, July 27 — Ignited by the ferocious baserunning of Andy Chun and the crafty pitching of Kerri Wheeler, the AT&T Goose-chasers won a resounding 16–6 victory last night over the powerful TSTech Blueshirts at TSTech Stadium. The victory was their first in four outings.

Buoyed by a nine-run outburst in the third inning, the 'Chasers played steady defense and took no mercy on the hapless TSTechers. Anchored by Chun at shortstop, the rock-solid infield of Ed Schiebel at first base (relieved in the third inning by Mike Christian), Mary Dupler at second base and Jianwei Lan at third base finessed everything the TSTechers hit at them. The outfield featured the speedy Glenn Houk in center, Gloria Rexing in deep left, and a determined Sushil Dravekar in right. Solid bench support was provided by Mary Lee Raines and the injured Mark McIntyre.

A pivotal moment came in the first inning when Sushil, a former cricket star in his native India, drove a low pitch into center field to score Rexing and Wheeler. Although it was the last low pitch he would see, Sushil continued his hitting rampage throughout the game, backed up by the torrid bats of Houk, Christian, Phil Warner, and Jianwei. Warner exacted revenge upon a pugnacious TSTech third baseman in the sixth inning with a bold, take-no-prisoners slide that left the swarthy TSTecher crying for his mama. Warner's triple proved to be the finishing touch of a relentless hitting onslaught.

Playing for her injured husband Mark, Sheri McIntyre caught a great game and proved to be a steadying influence on the mercurial Wheeler, who twirled a gem from the mound, limiting the TSTech team to six runs with a mix of slow, slower, and slowest pitches. After several innings of fruitless swings, the frustrated TSTech bench lapsed into a coma. The crafty Goosechasers took care not to wake the sleeping giant until the last out was recorded.

The 'Chasers next game (Monday, August 2 at 7 P.M.) will likely see the same lineup on the field, as their coaching staff is not likely to mess with a successful formula. This inspiring bunch have proven themselves to be the winning combination.

◆

TWO-OUT THUNDER:
GOOSECHASERS LIMP TO 2ND STRAIGHT WIN, 14–9
Skalski, Foley Injured in Winning Effort

REYNOLDSBURG, 3 August — The Goosechasers mounted another fine effort last night in defeating The Limited, 14–9, in a game marred by injuries to two key players.

During a seven-run first inning that saw five runs scoring with two outs, Goosechaser third baseman Pete Skalski drilled a line drive to left center field that skipped past the Limited's outfielders for a home run. Skalski injured his hamstring while rounding first base, but continued running all the way home before collapsing in pain on the plate. After the game, he was helped to a car, driven home and dumped into bed by teammates. Mrs. Skalski was not amused.

The injury suffered by Rod Foley, while judged to be less serious, had more of an air of mystery about it, as befits Sir Rod. After nearly being hit in the back of the head by a throw from center field, Foley limped away from third base clutching his leg in pain. He was helped to his car by his son, Ben Foley, and drove off for the hinterlands.

Meanwhile, the Goosechasers continued their winning formula of good pitching and fine defense. Kerrie Wheeler threw a solid game, and was backed by steady infield and outfield play. Of particular delight to the gathered throngs were a fine running catch in short right field by the galloping Ed Schiebel and consistent second base play by the coy Mary Dupler. On the offensive side, fair-haired Glenn Houk led the 'Chaser attack with three hits, hard-hitting Gloria Rexing contributed four base knocks, Schiebel spanked a pair of key line drives and Dupler reached base every time she was up. Skalski's home run capped the seven-run first; the 'Chasers also mounted two-out rallies in the second, third, and sixth innings. Of their 14 runs, 10 were scored with two down.

Other contributors included quick-footed Andy Chun at shortstop and third base, rock-solid Tom King at third, the slick-fielding Mike Christian at first, steady-eyed Sheri McIntyre catching, the aging Jerry Kelly at shortstop, and fan-favorite Yoli Albright* in right center field. Mark McIntyre was seen testing his new keep-the-arm-in-the-shoulder-socket harness on the sidelines before the game, and is expected to return as a first baseman in the next two weeks. Shortstop Felipe Brooks is reported to be ending his holdout and may return to the team soon, though team officials are uncertain how "The Big Crybaby" will be received by fans and teammates.

Onlookers have noted how the Goosechasers seem to be solidifying into a solid defensive unit. They've been making most of the routine plays in the field, thus denying opponents those long, error-scarred innings that usually characterize recreational softball. With Wheeler on the mound and a revolving cast of characters playing superb defense, the 'Chasers lack of big power hitters has not proven a hindrance these last two weeks. They hit and run the bases well enough to score runs, and their pitching and defense slam the door on opponents' hopes for big innings. The Goosechasers are proving themselves to be an interesting case study in effective team chemistry and "small-ball."

♦

— Original Message —

From: Skalski, Peter M, ALCOO

Hi Everyone,

I'm back, and want to thank you for the concern. The doc was merciless during the examination yesterday. As it turns out, I managed to tear my right medial hamstring. Crutches, darvocet, ibuprofen and bit of therapy to deal with, aside from the fact that I'm just a tad pissed about all of this. Perhaps it is time to hang up the cleats and move on to some other sports—darts, fishing, horseshoes, golf. Maybe become an ump or referee. (My wife has heard all of this before.)

Anyway, see ya around the campus.

Hurtin' but breathin',

Pete

♦

GEESE STEP LIGHTLY OVER TOWELETTES
Both Teams Cheerful in 12–5 'Chaser Win; Ump Tickled

REYNOLDSBURG, 23 August — The Goosechasers continued their winning ways last night with a well-played 12–5 victory over The Limited Towelettes. The game was remarkable for its good-natured competitive atmosphere and for the giddiness of the umpire, who seemed to be enjoying himself immensely.

'Chaser Catcher Lisa Stone may have lifted the umpire's good cheer into high gear when she attempted to wave to a young fan and inadvertently made contact with a portion of the umpire with which she was previously unfamiliar.

"His eyes got very big," a bystander commented.

The game itself offered plenty of good things to watch. Kerrie Wheeler pitched perhaps her best game yet, confidently feeding out-pitches to a succession of Towelette batters. Normally a good-hitting team, the Limiteds were limited to only a few hits off Wheeler's magic.

The 'Chasers continued to display the solid team defense that has jelled since early in the season. Mike "Big Smooth" Christian showed casual prowess at first base, pulling down linedrives and snagging grounders to both sides. He and Wheeler have developed impeccable timing on their first base coverage, using it last night to shut off several incipient Towelette rallies.

The game marked the return of injured Gander Mark McIntyre, who jumped back into the fray at third base and played remarkably well for one who almost lost a wing several weeks back. Mary Dupler returned to her second base duties after missing a week and made several nice plays in conjunction with Charles Alston, newly installed at shortstop. Fans witnessed another triumphant return in the person of Felipe Brooks, who patrolled left center field with the poise of a matador. Brooksie nonchalantly pulled down several long Towelette drives, and it appears his attitude is much improved after an early-season episode in which he refused to play because his shirt was too "baggy" and his shorts were too "long." It was obvious in the 'Chaser dugout that the team was glad to have the old Felipe back.

The one injury suffered in the game came when Ginny Blake pulled a quadriceps muscle while legging out a hard grounder. The Towelettes were kind enough to provide ice and a place to sit until Ginny could make her way back to the winning side.

Offensively, the Goosechasers resumed their usual pattern of long innings with runs coming in bunches. McIntyre and Wheeler led the attack with 3 and 4 hits, respectively, while newcomer Alston hit a two-run homer in the third and had a total of 4 RBIS. Fiery outfielder Gloria Rexing took the collar for the first time this season, but Christian contributed a decisive three-run homer in the sixth inning to ice the victory. Other significant contributors included Glenn Houk with three hits, Yoli Alston with two, and a key two-run double by the sly Stone during that long third-inning rally.

Speaking of catcher Stone, the umpire made a point of mentioning that he'd like to see her catch the All-Star Game. "I'll work behind her any time," he said with a Hollywood wink.

♦

— Original Message —
From: Kelly, Jerry, ALCOO

Howdy, all

Just a reminder that our final Goosechaser softball match is this coming Monday, 9/13, with an early start (5:15 P.M.). We play the mighty TSTech CupHolders, who defeated the first-place Cheeseballs two weeks ago. Come prepared to runneth them over!

♦

Chasers Finish with Style
Pitching, Defense, Timely Hitting Prevail
As 'Chasers Tip CupHolders, 12–7

Reynoldsburg, 13 September — With the sun setting on a fine co-ed softball campaign, it seemed appropriate that TSTech's left field was crowded with more than a hundred geese just prior to Monday's game. It was as if they had come to bid the Chasers farewell for the season. And before signing off, the Chasers gave the hissers something to honk about.

Led once again by the finesse of pitching ace Kerrie Wheeler and the hot bat of Mark McIntyre, the Chasers scored early and often. McIntyre scored in the first inning (knocked in by the free-swinging Ed Schiebel) while the Chaser defense held the CupHolders in check through the first three frames. McIntyre scored again in the third, along with Schiebel, knocked in by hits from the devoted Lisa Stone and agile shortstop Andy Chun. The Holders came back with a couple runs in the fourth inning, and true to form, the Chasers exploded in the fifth, scoring seven times as they batted through the order. This rally featured five consecutive hits by McIntyre, Wheeler, Schiebel, Stone, and Chun, followed later in the inning with singles by the emotive Mary Dupler and Chaser sparkplug and leadoff hitter Glenn Houk. The ever-graceful Gloria Rexing worked a walk to extend the rally, while plucky Sheri McIntyre contributed an RBI single an inning later.

On the sidelines, itty-bitty batboy Ben Foley warmed up for football season with his father, a former tight end for the U.S. Navy. Our other Navy vet, Pete Skalski, is still recovering but was willing to play if needed. Pete kept the scorebook and order in the ranks.

In a fitting climax to a truly sweet season, first baseman Mike Christian blistered his last pitch of the ballgame for what may have been the hardest-hit ball of the Chaser campaign. Impressed by the speed and trajectory of Mike's hit, the left field honkers took off in unison, forming a giant V-for-Victory sign in the sky while doing a formal flyover to salute the Chasers. At least, that's what onlookers hoped they were doing. But just to be on the safe side, most dove for cover under the picnic tables, or hoisted umbrellas if they had them. 'Cuz you never know what them birds might be thinking.

[Thanks for all the good times, everybody. It's been a fun season!
You did us proud.]

Gambier Ghosts

Legend rests its wrinkled hand upon Gambier, Ohio, and in particular the old college, which is riddled with ghost stories. It sometimes seems as if there are more spirits than living souls on Gambier
hill, especially in high summer when the students are gone and town-
ies take to lolling in the shade of their privately-haunted trees.

One vivid local legend is that of the fraternity pledge tied to the
Baltimore & Ohio railroad tracks back in 1905 as a hazing prank, his
so-called brothers knowing full well that no train was scheduled that
night. When an unscheduled freight rumbled through and slaughtered
the poor kid, horror and scandal ensued. A weight of shamed notori-
ety hung over Kenyon for years; the college historian reported being
asked by someone in 1976, "do they still tie kids to the tracks there?"
And ever since, new freshmen have been lured onto late-night walks
down by the old rail bed and told the story of poor Stuart Pierson and
how his faint terrified cries creep up the hill from the long-gone tracks
on certain nights—most often courtesy of other frat-boys hiding
behind their own self-haunted trees.

Kenyon's ghosts are known far and wide, the legend dispersed by
generations of alumni and wide-eyed visitors. Over time, the tortured
spirit of Stuart Pierson (who, according to the official college history,
"fell asleep on the tracks during a fraternity initiation") and those of
the victims of the Old Kenyon fire of February 1949 have found their
way through the woods, cemeteries and ballfields within earshot of
their gruesome, long-gone but ever-present endings.

◆

Weekly community softball games have been a perennial Gambier summer pastime ever since anyone remembers. Our version
emerged with a lively spirit of games past in the summer of 1995. We
played easy softball within whistling distance of the hill, just down in
the valley beside a cornfield, every Tuesday evening. We'd meet at 6:30

behind the old elementary school (now the village hall and polling place) to play ball on a big dirt infield. This community ballfield — the larger of two there behind the old school — has base posts set for both baseball and softball. You can anchor the bases 65 feet apart for softball or little-league ball, or 90 feet apart for the larger ballgame of baseball. Unfortunately, this dual-sized, all-purpose setup makes the community field a neither/nor proposition; there's no mound for baseball, but instead a flat pitching slab at 60 feet or so; a softball pitching rubber is set in front of that, at 45 feet from home plate. Repeated efforts to maintain a baseball mound have been zeroed out by the volunteer caretaker who smooths the infield by dragging an old bent section of chain link fence behind his pickup truck, around and around in circles, shaving the mound right away. The skin infield is a festival of bad hops — tire tracks, mud ruts, and loose gravel from the last ice age.

The lack of a pitching mound takes away a pitcher's power, so elemental to balanced baseball; between that factor and the hippity-hoppity infield surface, it's not hard to see that this is a hitter's park. The outfields are huge, back to a tall tree line in deep right that fades deeper toward center, disappearing beyond the playground. The smaller ballfield sits out in deep dead left.

Our skin infield is large for softball, but cramped for baseball; either way you play it, it's less than ideal. Before our Gambier Indians' home games there, we line everyone up and march them slowly across from the third-base line to the second-base line to fill their hats with stones. It's soldierly duty, very American. The guy (or usually, the cabal) collecting the biggest pile of rocks gets free cans of soda-pop after the game, which is sufficient incentive to set off frantic competition amongst them, with elbowing and outright theft all part of the reckoning. There's never any shortage of stones as fuel for this economy.

♦

While the 13- to 15-year-old Indians proved to be righteously faithful in their game-day attendance, we never knew who'd show up at the community softball game on any given Tuesday. It was usually a mix of local guys who'd played some organized ball in their time but no longer played in real leagues — professors, college staff workers, locals. Some Kenyon students joined the set, seemingly more adept at golf and tennis; and a few women who wanted to mix it up with the guys or had been coaxed into doing so. The occasional small kid would be placed out of harm's way in deep right field or behind the fence, and of course, given his swings.

We'd count off to form teams and lope out across the dirt to play some easy innings. No one kept score. The point was not winning, but playing. There was a sense of jubilant anarchy about it; opponents cheered and jeered each other with equal glee. Everyone was a star in some way, in their moment. And if one struggled to keep up, the game would slow down, the whole scattered group pausing like settlers crossing a wide prairie toward a new home, waiting for the last wagon to catch up. It was, by turns, touching and heroic and comic, and very good-natured. There was a sense of rightness and justice about it; everyone was included and given their moment to shine. A laugh counted more than a run in this sweet carnival.

◆

After several seasons of its vivid, happy democracy enduring, the intrusion of the ghosts into the community softball game took place gradually. Because they arrived in my absence, the ghostly change in the character of the game seemed sudden to me, but I'm supposing it happened slowly. I'd become an exile in my fourth summer in Ohio, with a new job 45 miles away keeping me from easily joining the Tuesday evening fray. An entire season passed without my attending a single game.

Toward the very end of that summer, with only a week or so remaining before the return of the college students and the end of the community softball season, I got a note from the new, self-appointed Commissioner, pleading — humorously but earnestly — for past and present players to make a showing for the final game. I left work early that Tuesday and buzzed home to get my gear and go down to play.

The ghosts were there when I arrived. They'd taken over. The game was forming up on the small pee-wee field, where adults normally coax five-year-olds through the fidgeting chaos of tee-ball. Unlike the skin baseball/softball field on the far side of the park, this little field is rutted with clumps of grass and weeds, and is so tiny that these men looked like giant little boys absent their fathers for the first time. As I walked up, I was struck by how the scene looked oddly compressed, devalued and just plain wrong—the community game gone all to hell, guided by ghosts closer to the eternal ditch of mortal absurdity.

The pool of players was now more homogeneously drawn: all men, most in their thirties and early forties, a few older. The women and children had disappeared, as if spooked away. There were just enough guys for a 9-on-9 game; teams jostled into order in a sorting process similar to what we'd done as kids, only now age-old resentments seemed to factor in. As I looked them over, feeling detached, I saw a gathering of ersatz occasional athletes raising competitive stakes between themselves with a nerdy sort of verbal joisting. As focused as they were on political positioning, they were clumsy and unskilled in their warmup throws, a bunch of howdy-doodies. A single player stood out as a quiet, authentic meat stick—Stan (The Man) Stauffer from the college print shop—the only guy who looked like he knew what he was doing in his own body. The others represented themselves convincingly as having never played competitively in their youth, now determined to talk a big game and blunder through a small one, oddly giddy and gawky.

Absent the girls and kids, the whole tone of the community game had changed. It was now an ongoing argument, good-natured but more than casually caustic, and driven to win by devilish ghosts chasing never-glimpsed glories. Each batter in turn tried to bash the ball into dust, lunging hard and lumbering off toward first as popups flared up and weak grounders dribbled out. The only exception was Stan the Man, who stepped to the plate each time and waited for the outfielders to fall back twenty yards. His powerful lefty coil at the plate bore the heavy grace of your classic slow-pitch softball slugger: he unwound it with quick and mighty torque and a very sound eye, his hands hitting frightful drives far over the outfielders' heads. With each of his at-bats, the rightfielder dropped back another ten yards, 'til he was standing in the skin infield clear across the park. Stan the Man just muscled up a little more each time, sending that rightfielder scampering back to retrieve another mammoth shot from the windblown corn of the great beyond.

♦

Naturally, my own phantoms came around to haunt me that evening. Having taken the summer off from baseball, working the office job and spending too many hours sitting in front of a computer screen, I was wobbly and weak, far out of game-shape even for softball. Ghosts of injuries past poked at my ribs and teased my knees, and so I throttled back, jogging rather than sprinting, feeling only halfway in this contest, with a scant whisp of game-drive echoing in the hollows of my ears. The field felt crowded with jeering spirits, unable to settle. It was a fog of experience with none of the sharp glare of a real game, either internally (in my muscles) or outwardly (in my play). I felt like the dead man walking, more akin to the seared spirits than the living souls lolling here beside me in their shadows.

The final straw — my only tangible souvenir of that game — was the sprained foot I suffered when the first baseman inexplicably jumped in front of me on the baseline as I jogged toward first. I have no idea what he was doing, nor did he — his jittery eyes were jumping elsewhere. I pulled up quick to avoid plowing him and came up lame. My left foot ached for a week, and I limped with the sullen gait of a chained wraith. Community softball had crossed over into oblivion, and winter was coming.

Fieldwork

Baseball diamonds decorate the American landscape abundantly, instantly recognizable from above and variously faceted at their surface. If you fly virtually anywhere over the U.S. in daylight, you can gaze down from your window seat and count them. They surround schools, define parks, and articulate neighborhoods. Sometimes singly, sometimes in clusters, diamonds bring you to ground from five miles up, giving you reason to believe that a soft landing will deliver you back to a reasonable sense of place. Local, humble and real, too small to serve as airfields but adequate as launching pads for a young slugger's rocket shots, America's diamonds testify that life can be that way — that even a poor young life can find its share of riches by creating them with physical imagination.

The wealth is about as evenly distributed as the ball diamonds. Which is not to say there's a direct correlation — only that, where you find diamonds, you locate the possibility of the game's essential richness. It takes effort and imagination to put a ballfield to best use, to maintain it (however rough its cut) as a field of potentials. On a baseball field, imagination and memory collide to create something new. The renewal of those possibilities is what gives a diamond significance.

The standard layout and dimensions are outlined in the official Rules of Baseball, complete with carefully-drawn schematics. But ballfields come in all shapes and sizes, within and without that geometry. Under ideal conditions, home plate points in a west-southwest direction; the imaginary line from catcher to pitcher to second base runs east-northeast. This is meant to minimize the effect of sun-glare on the game. But not all fields are so situated. From the air, you can see that they point every which way.

To an extent, what surrounds a diamond defines it — as a retroluxe new stadium or a faded haunt; a high-school playing field on a wide suburban plain or an empty lot squeezed between city buildings; a rock-strewn potato field or, like State, a sump with household debris scattered along its periphery and put to use in defining its form. The point is, a diamond is emblematic; its surface reflects its locale, brightening it over time with the passage of a small spinning ball. Regardless of what lies beyond, within a diamond the game is all.

Walking across a baseball field, pausing to look around, you can feel dislocated, strangely out of place; but running across it after a ball, the measures make sense and feel quite right, and the eyes only see as far as open ground permits and lines extend — only as far as the game can go.

When it comes to playing on local fields, the sheer variety can be maddening. One week you're on a smooth dirt surface (called a "skin" infield for what it gives and what it takes); the next you're on unmowed, clumpy grass. One game on a fine green pool table, the next in a minefield. Strafed and bombed, we used to say. My city-kid friends played on asphalt — sliding and diving on abject pavement dazzled with bits of broken glass, leaving some serious skin behind. It's the game all the same, diversified in its rough edges.

Emblematic, a diamond reaps what is sown (yielding, in legal terms, something akin to a farm-field's emblements); efforts put to making a field fit can boost the crop. Over State, we cranked hijacked lawnmowers and swung rusty scythes to bring our swampy sump closer to form; we planted grass one seed at a time in the vain hope of recreating the green vectors of Yankee Stadium. Later, we put rakes and shovels and buckets to use in draining water and scraping mud from other soaked infields. Such labors allow games to succeed under less-than-ideal conditions. And sometimes desperate measures bear unexpected fruit.

One rainy night, as we labored over a soppy infield trying to get our Cardinal game in, I watched a local genius click his cleats across the parking lot to his truck and lift a dented five-gallon gasoline can from the back. As he lugged it bow-legged back to the field, we paused on our rakes and shovels; then we watched him unscrew the cap. When he commenced wildly slinging the gas onto the infield mud, spinning on his heel and broadcasting shiny arcs of it into a more-or-less even coating across the field surface, we stepped back. When he began digging in his jacket pocket for a book of matches, we retreated to the dugouts and watched him stomp from puddle to puddle, flicking them into small explosions and standing back to watch them burn. His face showed the rage of genius in the dancing firelight. One by one, we gathered our manhood and emerged to join in the conflagration. To this day, the vision of twenty ballplayers strolling amidst flaming puddles is an oddly-enduring one. The madman's plan worked — his flames burned off the worst of the rainwater, and that toasted dirt infield hosted a righteous game that night. I slugged a home run off Angelo Pepitone and jogged all around that burnt circuit with my head down, replaying those flames and the hot-knife-through-butter sensation of that swing. Whatever else might go up in smoke, that moment remains.

All rituals enacted to recover a playing field share a characteristic craze, a scramble to create occasion from neglect, to raise the figure of a diamond from layers of mud. Time and again I've seen ballplayers work like canal diggers, putting their backs to the task of channeling water. I've been one of those earnest mules, more times than I wanted to be. But often enough our efforts yielded game — perhaps mud-sloppy and slippery — or caked dry and dusty-brown — but game nonetheless. Professional turf men manicure big league fields to create the ideal; kids with balky lawnmowers and men with gasoline imagine something more.

♦

To get to the very crux of it, a ballfield begins at home plate. Picture a white 17-inch square with the two rear corners clipped off to form a point. Its flat, field-facing edge is 17 inches straight across; the sides square off and fall back for 8.5 inches, then angle in as converging 12-inch lines to the point at the back of the plate. That point is the fulcrum of the game; it arrows straight back through the catcher to the umpire. Not from the front of the plate, but from that rear point forward to the pitching rubber measures the sacred sixty feet, six inches. Home plate sits squarely thus in fair ground, while outward from the rear point run the 90-foot basepaths—first base to right, third base to left. The game moves that way, from right to left; baserunners become experts of the hard-leaning left turn, around first motoring for second, around second turning for third, and hard around third heaving for home. In all, it's a sprint of 120 yards from home to home—the length of a football field and then some, with three hard-leftward turns. It's not for the faint of heart.

In miniature, then, home plate figures the field of play; a 12-inch square turned 45 degrees within a 17-inch square; a 90-foot square within a big open field; an inner diamond defining an outer one, scaling up to distances fit for human legs and desire.

Home plate is the starting and ending place for all else occurring on a baseball field. It's the hotspot from which players and plays arc out—the focal point for all defense arrayed to defeat each batter. The moment-by-moment progress of a game crosses home plate with each pitch (or fails to cross it, or puts unhittable strikes at its edges, in and out, high and low, fast and slower). With a game-tying runner bearing down from third, the catcher setting for a throw and bracing for a hit, the rightfielder firing a bullet to the cut-off man, who turns sideways to catch and afterburn it with a homeward peg—for a game's final out—or the runner's twisting slide to keep it all going—the play at the plate is a singular instance of what a flashing diamond can reflect.

♦

The strike zone emanates invisibly upward from the plate to form a column at a floating height that begins at the hollow of a batter's knees and extends up to his armpits, or letters, or belt-buckle, depending on who's calling balls and strikes. That hovering volume of air and light doesn't exist without a specific batter crouching in the box, looking for a pitch, and with an umpire crouched behind him, seeing balls and strikes in his own way. The strike zone is the game's grail and its port of entry. As a player, you work to command it from one side or another — from the pitcher's mound sixty feet in front of it, or from either side's batter's box, or from behind as a catcher or umpire. It's the window you have to crawl through (see through, swing through, throw through) to keep the game going your way.

The best way to size up a ballfield is by standing over home plate, looking out. You can get it all by taking a good long look, then lowering yourself to your batting crouch and taking it all in, then lowering more to a catcher's crouch for the whole big view. Below this line of sight is the surface itself — a mix of dirt and clay, or red brick dust on the best fields. The infield can be dirt all the way, or grass and dirt — like a carpet or like rubble. You take whatever it gives.

From the strike zone outward, a ballfield's surface rises up to claim you, for good and bad. No one gets out of it without experiencing some of both. The gifted, articulate Yankee outfielder Bernie Williams said it this way: "Baseball is a very humbling game. Just when you think you are big and nobody can get you out, you go into a slump and everybody gets you out. You are always dealing with failure, it seems. In a single game you can go from feeling exhilarated, excited, feeling like you are bigger than the whole world, and then end up feeling like dirt."

"Like dirt," he said. The very stuff upon which bad hops, base hits and great plays are made.

◆

State had all the best and worst of it. The moist, salty clay fostered strange mosses, but not grass. We picked pebbles eternally but never got them all; broken bottle shards likewise. The stream in mid–right field was usually dry, but sometimes flowed with rain water channeled from the surrounding streets or trickling down through the hillside. The scraggly hill itself, steep and rutted with washouts, gave us the sense of enclosure essential to our stadium mind, but made it tough on rightfielders. The entire place was a bastion of bad hops, yet it gave up glorious play like rich loam gives up mushrooms. Although it remains the most challenging field I've ever played upon, I somehow managed to avoid getting hurt on it, losing teeth and tendons elsewhere on rich green turf. All the spring, summer and fall days spent playing ball over State added up to real comfort and skill upon that broken ground, knowing it like the skin knows sunlight.

The best surface I ever played on was the Seattle Mariners' spring training complex in Tempe, Arizona, where we played MSBL tournament games in the late 1980s. We tried to find a bad hop anywhere on the Tempe Diablo Stadium infield, but couldn't. I was amazed at how the smooth playing conditions helped everyone's confidence in the field. Our innings there seemed to flow with a rich grace and crisp, grateful energy.

But a diamond's defined by what surrounds it, and for that, my favorite playing field was Ocala, Florida's, Gerig Park, the old spring training haunt for the New York Giants (and later, the Boston Red Sox) where we tried out for the Indianapolis Clowns in 1990. What surrounds Gerig is a poor neighborhood known locally as Westside — a long way from hope in the third-world sort of way, peopled with generations of black kids raised on sandy soil in heavy air. Some of them lived to dream of playing inside Gerig's high walls, and through the years, as the big leaguers abandoned the crumbling park, these kids took it over and became enduring heroes upon it, learning to win and lose on hallowed ground. What they realized there epitomizes the local, essential American pastime: the ground-spring, one particular vital source of all that flows together — creeks and streams feeding rivers — running to the mighty baseball oceans. Across such fields the game truly runs, its diamonds glistening as you crane your neck from your window seat to take a look.

Vision

Watching a ballgame on TV can be maddening, because TV makes things disappear. Have you ever gone to a ballpark and taken your seat beneath an upper-deck overhang? Deep in that sheltered space you have the whole panorama of the field before you, but you can't see up. So when a flyball goes up, it goes completely out of your sight. In that instance, you do what managers do from the back of the dugout — you don't watch the ball, you watch the fielders. Their movements tell you where the ball is going, and lead your vision to what is about to happen.

With TV, we have a tragic subtraction of that: no panorama, no looking up or out of the frame, no looking anywhere but where a control-room director decides you should look. So, in a dramatic moment, an aging slugger belts a ball out of the park for a game-winning homer, and just as you want to see his whole circuit around the bases — to watch him conducting himself in his momentary glory, and see the young teammates pouring out of the dugout, and the pitcher staggering off the mound, and a manager hugging his clipboard — the game's dramatic panorama, complete — the director pans the crowd, showing you distant little people clapping. As if you can't hear them. As if he thinks fans want to see other fans, like monkeys might want to see other monkeys. In truth, we want to see the game — the whole game — and nothing but the game. TV, in its present form, does not allow for that. It's amazing how limited and limiting it is.

Here's what could improve things greatly: interactive TV with viewer control over what he or she is watching at any given moment. A lens on each player in the field, and one on the batter, and one on each baserunner, all available for the viewer to select. Tracked cameras down the first- and third-base lines to accompany the baserunners (like those now used in telecasting Olympic sprints and swimming). Let me switch from view to view at will, and see several at once, so I can observe what the first baseman is doing between pitches and the moment a ball is hit. Let me watch the on-deck batter in his ritual. Have cameras trained on each dugout so I can check in on the brain-trust now and again, maybe take a glance down the bench to watch the scrubs squirming. Show me the bullpens so I can catch the staff napping or hurry-up warming. Let me look where I want and see the whole game. Tell you this: I'd never, ever think I should pan the crowd.

Want to make it really appealing? Give me the option of not listening to the play-by-play from the booth, but instead to the ambient noise of the ballpark. I can see what's happening without the narrative filler; with present TV, I often turn off the sound to better understand the game. (Try it — it works.) Let me hear the crowd and see the whole vista. I'd be much more there than I presently am, watching a TV ballgame. The quality of my attention would be so much greater.

Commercials? I suppose we have to live with them. But it sure would be nice to be able to catch some between-inning action. Could we opt out of the commercial feed for an inning — maybe start by giving us the seventh-inning stretch, keeping us in the ballpark for that — or better yet, is there a way to present ads without completely losing the ballpark? In fact, using the ballpark. Present technology proposes answers to these issues.

Engage viewers in the game more by putting us in baseball time, which is out of time. The game plays out in expanded moments, without persistent measure; there's no clock except an incidental one marking the game's length. There's time and space for lots of banner ads, including virtual ones not seen in the ballpark, and for the game's thought to deepen. There's opportunity to hold viewers' attention more fully by letting them interact with the game in a way that really brings it home.

Open the idea of TV baseball more fully and pull us in by letting us interact with its complete occasion. That's something a viewer could love, and an advertiser should.

9

LEAGUE OF DREAMS

Co-Ed

Settling into life in Ohio, I became aware of certain differences between the people here and those I'd known in New York. We all accept these blazing generalities as truisms: New Yorkers are more contentious (to me, more up-front); Ohioans are more polite (to me, passive-aggressive). A New York minute is an Ohio hour. Time doesn't fly here, it stands on one leg.

It's evident in the way people drive. Ohio locals will ignore right-of-way rules to wave a driver over into their lane; they'll stop to allow an oncoming car to make a left turn against traffic (sometimes resulting in spectacular rear-end or head-on collisions). You also see it in fast-food restaurants: Ohio people will wait in line forever without a peep, even if the kids behind the counter are screwing around instead of waiting on their customers. The same scene in New York will quickly result in a shouting match or a food fight — at the very least, some loud, well-aimed, biting sarcasm. But here in Ohio, people stand in line silently, seeming not to suffer the passage of time like New Yorkers do.

It occurred to me (with a typical New York tilt) that this was the essential difference: people back home were descended from monkeys, while the Ohio branch of the species had clearly descended from the cows. If you've ever watched cows gathered in a field, chewing their cuds, you get the idea. On the other hand, if you're a midwestern type,

Market Dogs of Gambier, Ohio, 1999.

the New York monkey analogy works just as well — even if you've never been to the Bronx Zoo to watch them throwing dung at each other.

As a transplant, you find ways to fight the tension that results from being a monkey-brain in a cow pasture. There's little point in trying to turn cows into apes. Conflict yields little that's useful; it's best to simply throttle back and try to adjust to the slower pace and pointed smiles. But there are occasions when you chafe against the herd and tip a few cows, just for the hell of it. You might not know quite what you'll get when you stir them up; but sometimes, you'll take a good stampede over a cheerful collective coma.

◆

When the word went out for players, I heard it early. The word was co-ed, meaning softball for men and women together. A college staff team sponsored by Kenyon was forming up to play in a summer weeknight league under the lights in Mount Vernon, Ohio, just five miles down the road from Gambier hill. Summertime Ohio, sitting as it does in the far west of the eastern timezone, sees daylight past 9:30 P.M.; so night games enjoy a late twilight, the lights coming on only when evening deepens over the edge of nightfall. The prospect of local night-ball caught my interest, even though I was playing baseball in Columbus and coaching kids in the Knox County Baseball League. I couldn't get enough, I guess, figuring this co-ed commitment would be an easy one, a lot of laughs. And it was, eventually.

I showed up for the first practice down at the community fields, where our Gambier Indians games with the kids and community games with the ghosts had been taking place. But the co-eds weren't using either of the two ballfields; instead they were scattered across an open area behind the picnic shelter, a rutted field more apt for grazing cows than for ballgames. One woman was self-hitting bloops in the general direction of a herd of fielders standing deep in this field with arms crossed or hands on hips. The batter seemed somewhat distracted by the cigarette smoke in her eyes. It was not a happy sight — no organized delight in evidence.

Doing some stretches on the side to warm up, I just watched for a few minutes. It was a dismal spectacle: the batter couldn't get a flyball anywhere near the outfielders, who were passively holding their ground, not moving in to where the bloops were falling. Kathy Bebout, at the plate, kept trying to tank a ball far enough for one of them to make a move for it, but it wasn't happening. This exercise had all the energy of a sedated Holstein, the agreeable joy of a new grudge.

"Beebs" (as we came to know her) finally turned to me with a face pleading for relief and said, "Here — you hit." She proffered her bat and bucket of balls. I stepped up and took them, and when she showed no inclination to run out and join the fielders, I asked her, "You want to catch for me?" She shrugged.

I began hitting flyballs at the group, scattering them like crows before a shotgun. Now they had something to go for, yet they remained reluctant, walking rather than running, preferring to stroll over to pick a ball off the ground rather than catching it before it landed. They showed no quickness, and poor throwing form, and they stood with their gloves hanging at their sides. A few more flies and I stopped and called them all in.

They didn't want to come in, either. I waved and they stood there. I called to them, "C'mon in!" and they still hesitated. "Are we done?" one of them cried out. "We're done doing this!" I answered, and slowly they all began to walk toward me, looking vexed and puzzled.

The first question I thought to ask is, "Who's running this team?" But I didn't ask it, because it was apparent that no one was. At least, no one with a clue. So I said to them, "Listen — why don't we do some throwing to each other, and practice that a little." Their body language replied that they just wanted to go home, but with some gentle coaxing they took balls from the bucket and paired off. I set them up in two lines twenty feet apart so we could work on throwing in a team-like fashion. They had no sense of this, no self-organizing instinct; perhaps if we'd been playing a game, they'd know to walk out to positions; but here, at this prototypical practice, they were unsure of the rituals, knowing not where to begin.

It was like playing with little kids, but the fundamentals were neither fun nor mental. Like you see sometimes at company picnics and other semi-forced softball occasions, all effort was desultory — disconnected and random. The few guys present had some basic skills, but most of the women had trouble throwing straight or catching anything. Suz and I had once gotten a game up amongst a Scandinavian women's track team, and having never played, they'd done almost as well as these people (although the nords had been somehow set on the notion of running the bases from home to third to second to first). This would be an adventure of a different kind.

Every coach knows, you got to work with what you got. There was a sad side to that, in terms of this collection; but there's always that sense (the more useful sense) of working anyway, to get better no matter how good or how bad you are to start. That was the angle that appealed to me, so I went with it. And now at least they were facing each other and making some sort of occasion.

The throwing nightmares were many and various. Girls tend to throw off the wrong foot — throwing righty, they step with the right leg. This method offers no balance, power or purpose. So I began correcting them, one at a time, modeling the proper right-handed throw with the left leg leading. Difficult to master if you've always done it the other way, this lesson goes slowly for most. But one young woman had been doing it right from the very start, and it was Evelyn more than me from whom the others took the cue. Twenty minutes into this simplest of drills, most everybody was throwing better, reaching their target, and catching every other ball thrown to them.

Evelyn Smith had learned baseball from her brothers, and on game nights all that season she'd warm up by hurling a ball with her sons on the sidelines. She was what a scout would call solid — small and tough, feminine and able. In this practice Evelyn emerged as the first ray of hope among the womenfolk, and thereafter she set a tone encompassing fun and good ballplaying, never hesitating to make a good effort, and carrying some of the others along with her. She was a much-needed ingredient that first night and all to follow; something about her made it believable that this game could be played for fun, and won.

◆

After a half hour of just throwing, we set up a makeshift infield there on the pasture (I was afraid if we moved the group to one of the ballfields, a bunch would surely flee to their cars). Hitting soft grounders to this array of possible infielders, I startled them a bit by telling them to get their butts down as they bent over to catch a ball off the ground — for some, a big problem. Bend your knees, I told them; get your hands out in front of you. Stay low. Crouch in toward the ball. Go get it before it gets to you. They were not easily convinced of the wisdom of this until Evelyn demonstrated it, scooting in with a low hop for a bounder and springing to a throwing position as soon as she had it in her glove. Thank god for her, I thought.

With Evelyn's graceful help, the practice almost found some positive momentum. There was still an air of reluctance among a goodly number of the group, most definitely those few who had sort of set things up before I'd arrived and were a bit resentful that I'd taken over. But their stubbornness was mostly silent; no one stepped up to take back the coaching mantle, and a few (most importantly, Evelyn) saw it for what it was — better than what they'd been doing, and a way to get things together as a team. As if pulled by two magnetic fields, the group coalesced to what seemed strongest, or at least most determined. It was a start.

♦

The prospect of tugging this sleepy herd across the wide prairie of a full season would have been far less appealing had it not been for two other peripheral Kenyon characters. Phil Brooks lived up on Ward Street with his wife, Balinda Craig-Quijada; Bally taught modern dance at the college. A freelance writer, "Felipe" is a Chicago boy and a life-long Red Sox fan who still teams up with his father every year for a trip to Sox spring-training games in Florida. He's baseball through and through—a keen fan and a strong amateur athlete. His great good humor can make any occasion fun, and he blessed us with game sense and comedy, all loosely wrapped in one wry and wiry package. Dennis Howard was a friend of Felipe's—a bit older than me, whereas Phil is a few years younger. Dennis owned several bakeries in Columbus and was renting a professor's house in the village as a summer retreat. A big man, he bore all the grace of his younger baseball heroics—slower now, more deliberate, but with much more athletic articulation than most guys have in their fifties. And an easy laughter that kept the game's comedy in perspective.

As we got everyone together for more practice sessions, tentative competencies formed like new cells, then new organs. We persisted in working on what coaches like to call the "basic fundamentals," gradually finding the mix of positions that permitted us some consistency in making the routine plays. The triumvirate of Felipe, Dennis and me put our best effort into coaching those who responded in kind—Evelyn getting better and better, others learning how to make bodily adjustments and locate flow to intercept the flight of a softball. Our game's transmission would never allow for all-out drag-racing, but we learned as a group how to keep it on the road and make some miles.

Watching particular players develop offers up small delights, especially when they are adults, clearly out of their youthful learning groove. They do what they can, and as they do it, you watch and encourage; if nothing else comes across, fun is a useful bottom line. Even the reluctant ones catch the winning contagion, if not every time, at least once and again. Those ready to play find more of it than they'd had, propagating it gladly amongst themselves, catching it and dropping it, making that one great play they'd never made but now can claim as their own, evermore. The will to get better brings power to any ballgame as it multiplies among players. Shared effort sparks a kindred spirit, reflexively. Watching it go from one to another — shadowing the ball, as it were — you weave the net of team around a group in their moment, giving everyone something more than what they brought here.

There were certain tendencies we could not correct, and didn't try to. Rachel was a case in point — an eager young woman in her mid-twenties, able to run a bit, not afraid of the ball. Working intently to develop her eye in the outfield, she was trying to get better at seeing the ball off the bat, at judging its distance and direction, the better to catch it on a fly. It took a bit of time for her eyes to get it; judging flyballs is a spatial skill unlike most of what we normally do. She was catching on, though, and her method was unique in our collective experience. Standing there in the outfield ready to go, she'd take a quick visual bead on a flyball and immediately thrust her left arm — her glove hand — straight up in the air. Then she'd take off running, keeping the arm aloft the whole way as the rest of her pumped like mad in pursuit. She somehow timed her catches so she didn't have to bend that arm; she always seemed to catch a fly with it fully extended, the glove intersecting the ball like a net at the end of a long pole — or, like a radar dish. We started calling her Radar, and she didn't know why, but didn't ask. It was all pure Ohio: we wouldn't have told her anyway. The fond nickname stuck.

As we approached the start of the season — our first game — it was evident we had some strength and some holes in our defense. Dennis was solid at first base, but we had him at third, trying some of the women at first. George Kost, a lanky guy in his late forties who worked with the college maintenance crew, was proving to be a yeoman infielder; we worked him at third and short, and he could handle either position capably. A bit slow afoot but very game, George could get his body sideways when he had to, snagging grounders with his long-armed reach, throwing well from his knees when it came to that. Felipe (we

double-nicknamed him "Nomi" after the great Boston shortstop Gar-
ciaparra) was himself an able shortstop, and a sparkplug there, but we
had him in left center field, where his speed and good eye could take
charge. I played some outfield, and some short, and first base on occasion, and I caught whenever I could. Mostly I coached from the sidelines, trying to get innings for as many of our Kenyon Co-Ed Irregulars
as possible. As a group, we played as if this was a three-legged race;
each athlete seemed strapped to a companionable cripple, and the game
would lurch along with the speed and grace of the slower member.

Evelyn was good enough to play a sure infield, but she also had
some good foot-speed, so she usually patrolled center field. She and
Felipe would spread themselves apart a bit more than normal to cover
our weaknesses in left field and right. The other women were inter-
spersed: Deb Shelhorn at first base or second, Beebs in right field,
Shirley Lepley out there otherwise, Radar in left field or center. While
serious co-ed leagues follow strict gender rules—you must alternate
positions by gender, as well as the batting order — this league had softer
guidelines, demanding only that the batting lineup be alternated
man/woman. We could array our fielders as we wished, as long as we
had equal numbers of both out there.

Pitching was a dilemma. We had Jason, a fine competitive softball
player who'd pitched in serious men's leagues. Jason could really hurl.
Like other good arc softball pitchers, he could vary the height and spin
of the ball, keeping batters off-balance, coaxing them into hitting his
pitch. He was expert at avoiding a hitter's wheelhouse, and could spot
a quality strike when he had to. The dilemma was, he could also play
the hell out of shortstop or the outfield; the pitcher's spot was a place
we could use a woman, thereby boltering our defense elsewhere with
Jason. And we had a volunteer: Barb Mowery had the pitcher's gleam
in her eye. She wanted the ball.

Barb was one of the original team organizers. She'd helped get the
college to underwrite this enterprise, and the trunk of her car held our
supply of shiny new bats and the bucket of balls. She brought the game
with her, including an unfailing platter of fresh-baked cookies.

Barb was not an athlete, but she had the spirit of one. Her life was
not the easiest one ever lived; as she told it, her husband had been but-
terknifed to death at the wheel of his car by another woman's husband.

Barb had known her share of the troubles, as the old Irish would say, but she kept her lights on and shined in every practice, even as she had trouble getting her pitches to reach home plate.

She wanted the ball, and for all that, we wanted to give her the shot she deserved. In practices I caught her, laying down some simple guidelines—the most basic form of a pitching regimen. She listened and tried to follow, wobbling on track as she struggled with her hips, legs, shoulders and long fingernails to deliver purposeful pitches.

She was just beginning to find some confidence when we got her in her first (real) game, and it quickly came undone. I knew her feeling, having had it in my first games as a young pitcher. You get moonie-eyed out there — the field swirls just a bit — and, because you're in the middle of it all, you tend to spin around, and over the course of an inning you can get a bit dizzy for it. You find yourself wobbling and wondering why, and it's very distracting. In Barb's case, her fingernails proved too much for any other discipline to overcome. I was catching, and could hear the ball scraping off her nails as she released it. The results were more like fingernails across a chalkboard. Her pitches were well short and flying to either side; unable to throw a strike, she quickly walked the first guy (who, under Co-Ed rules, walks not to first but to second base); the next batter in the lineup, a woman, then has the choice to take an automatic walk, or to take her swings. This binary rule prevents co-ed pitchers from intentionally walking the men to pitch to only the women; but it also skews the offense, because if a pitcher starts walking a few batters, you've quickly got a conga line crossing home plate.

Barb walked off the mound before she'd dug us in too deep. I'd never allow one of my players to do that under game circumstances, but this was different; Barb was crumbling. No need for such scenes to devolve into trauma; bottom line, this wasn't fun for her, but we'd want her to try again soon. We ushered her into the dugout and put her in charge of keeping the scorebook, then rearranged the defense to get Jason back on the mound.

And we battled. Surprising ourselves, we were winning these games, taking our first five without a loss. The competition was truly pathetic, and the holes in our defense were not so big that these other stalwarts could drive a game through them. Our basic fundamentals were working well enough to beat really bad teams, and so we sat back and enjoyed it, fielding a mix of our best and worst and going for broke. Through it all, we took the approach that we'd win by minimizing our own mistakes while allowing the opposition to compound their own. Our most common and urgent call was "hold the ball!" — knowing that, by not making those desperate, low-percentage throws, we'd be less likely to throw it away. Training our fielders to resist making those throws lessened the number of runs we gave away; better to hold the ball and let one runner score than heave it and let three in. It took awhile for the message to sink in, but as we watched other teams make one errant throw after another (as we circled the bases) we began to get the idea.

On defense, we emphasized getting one out at a time. Other teams would go for the edgy doubleplay, and get no one; we drilled our infielders in dropping to one knee to catch a grounder and making one good, short throw to get the easiest out. Often, the easiest out was the lead runner. Deb Shelhorn got very good at making those routine plays. Time and again, we shortened the other teams' rallies by getting one out at a time at second base. And most often, after making 18 of those routine plays, we'd have ourselves a win.

After five of these basic, workmanlike victories, we were gaining some real confidence. Going into our next doubleheader we were swaggering — undefeated! — but another stalwart we called "The Pill" had been lobbying hard for a pitching start, and he was wearing down our better judgment. Jason had gotten us through this run of early victories with brilliant pitching and fielding heroics, but The Pill wasn't buying this Team thing — he wanted some glory for himself. We finally relented and gave him a start in the first game of a doubleheader, and thus experienced our first good whomping of the season. His pitches were flat and uninspired, with opposing women batters ripping linedrives everywhere, the men hitting bombs, burying our fielders under a flurry of hits. The Pill kept insisting he was fine, he'd get the next one out; boom — kaboom — kaboom — the shelling continued. The game was soon out of reach, and our undefeated status gone to ashes. The team's body language in the dugout after the first game hung low, reeling a bit from the pounding we'd taken, our invincibility now truly gone. But we rallied the troops, fielded our best to open the nightcap, and pounded them early. Our retribution didn't let up, and I was quietly very pleased to see that we didn't like losing, and felt we deserved to dish out some just desserts. This opponent was the best we'd faced, but they weren't that good; they were beatable, and we proved it to them and ourselves with a rousing, raucous comeback in that second game.

Meanwhile, The Pill sat sullen on the sidelines. He hurt us there too, draining a measure of fun out of victories. He always wanted to pitch, but could dig us a hole on the mound faster than that monster machine that bore the English Channel chunnel (too big to back out, they simply turned it sideways and let it bury itself — unfortunately, we had not that option with The Pill). Even playing catch on the sidelines, he could hurt us; he'd snap his head as he threw, never looking the ball to where he was throwing, always heaving it too hard; even if we were ten feet apart he'd whip it with all his might (Pill was about 6' 2", pushing 230). Athletically, he had what we call a football mind, which is almost no mind at all — reptilian in its best moments.

Our women, as it turned out, resonded best as a group, pulling together under this rubric of winning ways. We pressed to get everyone playing time, but when winning takes hold, you go with your best to keep it going. Several of the women were having to sit some innings, and they generally took it well.

The men were another matter. The Pill was always pleading his case, sometimes like a jailhouse lawyer, sometimes with silent, sullen looks. His chances at third and first were utter failures; he was twitchy with nervous eyes, and he threw too hard for most of the women (and some of the men) to handle. Holding the ball was not in his game plan.

Byron was another tough one. A young preacher, he had a way of creating panic in the congregation when we put him in left field. In one instance, we had a five-run lead before Byron's hurtful pout in the dugout finally wore us down and we put him in. In no time he got us behind the eight-ball by heaving a base hit from short left over the entire infield, allowing three runners to score and shaving our lead to a deuce. Huddled in the dugout, Felipe, Dennis and I began referring to such plays as Byronical. A walking catastrophe as a player, he could not hit a cutoff man to save his life; the ball would inevitably find him, and he never failed to heave it over everyone's head. But Byron was pious, and he always apologized, though he never truly made amends. He once stopped on his way to first and expressed his solemn regrets to a third baseman after hitting a line drive past her for a single, thus almost getting himself gunned out at first base by the leftfielder. He was truly sorry. And so were we, whenever we caved in to his homilies.

Tony Steinz* was our big strong guy. He wanted to tear the cover off the ball with every swing, but popped up a lot, and so spent time on the bench. Even the faint pressure of a co-ed softball game can crackle with enough static to make some players stiffen when the ball comes their way. For The Pill, Byron and Troy this was clearly the case, and in the dugout we tried to mediate their feelings of rank injustice by promising them their chance to get in there. To his credit, Troy was much better than Pill or Byron at staying in the game and cheering his team from the sidelines, and we got him more at-bats for that.

Of our femme regulars, Evelyn and Radar and Lynn Clark became very solid players. They made the routine plays wherever we put them, and Lynn was positively heroic behind the plate, hanging in there like Thurman Munson with a runner bearing down and a throw coming in. As Felipe said, all you have to do as a fielder is show her the ball before you throw it, and she'll catch every one. With two cutoff pegs from him to her in one game, they turned both plays into key outs at the plate. Show her the ball and throw it, and she'll catch it and make a clean sweep tag every time. She always came up grinning.

Deb Shelhorn started strong but gradually came unwound over the course of the season. She was nursing the small bouquet of injuries that can follow you through a season, and her confidence ebbed. Her folks showed up at every game with their lawnchairs, just as they had when Deb was a kid. They set the chairs as close to the edge of the field as they could, just barely in foul ground, and her father would bellow instructions at her the whole game in a steady cadence — "Get yr arm up — drop yr head when you're running!" I think it gradually wore her down.

Beebs, finally, was the epitome of our co-ed squad. Never relenting on her claim to being nominally in charge, she played whatever innings she wanted in right field, and insisted on her at-bats. She was not one to sit still for being benched, but would take herself out of games on occasion to sit and smoke with her fans in the bleachers. Her most memorable play came on a ball hit to the right-field fence in a losing effort late in the season; when she got to it she pulled up to a sudden stop and backed away in horror. She stood there pointing at the ball while the runners rounded the bases unimpeded. Turns out there was a large, bright-green tomato worm near the ball — not on it, but near it — and she was having none of that. Beebs' devotion to this enterprise found its absolute limit in that worm, and so Rachel finally had to run over from center field to retrieve the ball. Beebs sat herself down for a restorative smoke as soon as that inning was over.

Glory came our way at the end of the season, in a game against Jacinda Rager's team — a very good co-ed team that battled every year for the championship of the stronger division. Our weak division had mercifully few games against that other one, and our pending game with The Jacindas had been the subject of bragging rights all season long. She was a terrific ballplayer, a rangy outfielder with keen instincts, a great drop on the ball, and the ability to cover ground. She could run down a gapper and catch it with the best of them, and always hit her cutoff. The rest of her team was about as good — women who'd played fast-pitch in high school or college, and guys crossing over from the men's leagues to complete the roster. As a team they were very solid, and in truth they played on a different level than we did. But the beauty of virtually any level of ball is that, on any given night, one team can find a way to beat another. The best team does not always win, and in this penultimate game we rose to the occasion. Luck was surely on our side; our bloops fell in, while their drives found our gloves. We played above ourselves for a night, and from the third inning on, after battling back from a first-inning deficit, we could smell victory. They took us for granted, spotted themselves a lead and then shifted into cruise control and gave it back; by the time they realized they could lose, we had all the momentum and would not give it up. We spanked them, winning by a comfortable margin and celebrating with quiet style and confident grace in the end — no whooping it up for this classy bunch. The Jacindas were crushed, and walked off the field with bad blood and blame brewing between them. There was no excuse in losing to us, except that we found a way to put our own excuses away and carry the day. No matter how small a season, no matter how humble an effort is possible, such wins take on a radiance in memory, outlasting all fact to the contrary. A sweet, sweet win such as this was the payday for working those fundamentals 'til they were basic, and putting teamwork on a pedestal as the be-all, end-all, co-ed beauty.

In retrospect, we were neither as good nor as bad as we variously thought we were. Going into the league playoffs full of determined confidence, we took a hard beating at the hands of a better team from the stronger division. It happened so quickly — we had no time to recover our sense of who or where we were. This team knew better than to give us any hope of finding any momentum; their attack was relentless until the final out was had. Give them credit, I said in the dugout afterwards; they did what they had to do. They knew we'd come back and beat them if they let down even a little. That's how the game is won at any level. In the end, winning this playoff game was not the point; we'd already won plenty. It was easy to see, and easy to accept, that we'd had more moments in the sun than we might have otherwise had — and none undeserving. We took our outs one at a time, and we held the ball. Monkeys and cows can evolve.

Lost & Found

We were sitting drinking beer in a booth at the Village Inn when the conversation came around to what's been lost. We got there by way of what we'd found as kids, growing up in specific places, playing various forms of ball. That's what we were discussing in this back corner of the dining room at the VI — a question of what, exactly, might be found by a young boy working his way into his body and life by throwing balls around. And what's been lost now amongst young boys whose time is programmed by parental constructions of "organized" "youth" "activities."

It was just me and Mitch Swaggert, the star of the resurgent Kenyon Lords. In his senior year, coming off shoulder surgery last spring, Mitch has lost little and somehow found a lot at Kenyon, leading the Lords with his devastating lefty changeup, electrifying center-field dives and whip-crack bat. More than that, it's been his winning attitude, reasoned and reasonable in its solidity. He's set a certain tone and paved a winning way for the star-crossed Lords.

For me, growing up, it was the Gladstone Gladiators then the Gorillas, and on and on. That was where I found the game. The neighborhood teemed with kids; we had our blessed sandlot sump we called State. We found the right ways to play, and settled things amongst ourselves with no adults involved — none present in that part of our lives, all those seconds and throws and minutes and innings and hours and games, those growing seasons. The parents ruled other scenes, surely, but not that one. The occasional father who came by to watch us play seemed awed by what we'd organized there, and was granted no opportunity to intervene.

Mitch grew up in downtown Minneapolis without many immediate neighborhood friends, so for him it was solo stoopball when opponents could not be mustered. Stoopball is best played with one or two others, but a form of it can be managed alone, and it's there (alone but not lonely) that skills get honed to sharp edges.

Stoopball is played against a stoop, requiring but a few of the lower steps. The ball is rubber — a Pennsy Pinkie or a Spalding or a tennis ball, or any other small and lively one. The pitcher stands a few feet in front of the steps, winds up (or runs up) and slings the ball against the edge of a step as hard as he can, with sharp aim. If he hits a step edge exactly, the ball jets off like a crackling line drive. If he has a fielder behind him, that guy has to track and catch said liner, along with all popups and bloops and medium-deep flies and grounders, using whatever space is available — the yard, street or alley — negotiating whatever impediments exist. Otherwise, the pitcher does it all himself — pitching from further back, fielding all comebackers. Stoopball finds itself in particular places. Thousands of variants employ the front porches of urban brownstones, back-door alleyway steps behind the bakery or schoolyard walls and canyons, and the sheer physical surge of youth. For Mitch, it was the front porch of his house, where he'd spend hours in solo practice, refining his windup, claiming his aim, and diving into imaginary bleachers to rob invisible hitters of real home runs.

I smiled at his description of this private version of stoopball. An essentially private guy, he seemed to take delight in relating it — and I was struck smiling by the familiarity of it all to my pitching against the fieldhouse wall. He would have gladly included others, but more often carried the whole game on his own shoulders. What's been lost? On him, none of that; it's recovered again and again in game situations here with the Lords, at home with his summer townball team, and on and on. His stoopball moves remake the game's occasion in other forms, a soul focus reimagining flow in muscle memory. He's known by what he carries, what he's found, and what it shows.

What lost? Certainly not belief. And here's a thought relating to our present-day Major League Baseball and its best players: were all those Dominican kids squired around by soccer moms to appointed rounds of so-called organized sport? Or did they find ways— stoops and sumps— sticks and stones— to realize the game in its own time, by their own rules and reckoning? How do they reach those Caribbean major league camps? Is it not by finding what we found over State or in the front yard, alone or in self-styled teams? Not lost on those kids, organic forms of ball guide young eyes into the trance and yield opportunities for diving into real bleachers to rob long-imagined home runs.

Market Dogs

Every picture tells a story, but most team portraits are sadly mute. Essentially group mugshots, team photos represent the ultimate in posed existential nothingness. Revealing little of a team's personality, its strength or weaknesses, its leaders and followers, its heroes and would-be's, most team photos capture a certain light falling across an anonymous uniformed bunch, arranged in rows and grimly holding forth as if pretending — or wanting — to be invisible.

On team photo day for the Gambier Village Market Indians, a harried photographer rolled up to the community field, scrambled out of his van and quickly herded everyone into the shade for their reluctant sitting. He'd obviously done it many times before; hired to photograph all of the teams in the league, he wanted this to go quickly, and knew how. Barking commands, he swiftly sorted us by size into the requisite rows— tall guys lined up in the back, then the mediums sitting on a bench in the middle, with the shorties crouching down in front. He set up his camera tripod while arranging us, deftly handling his gear without even glancing at it. He lifted his hand and snapped his fingers to point each player into place, using his commanding voice to hold our attention and secure passive compliance. The results of his enterprise were predictable: in our official team photo, the faces show some thin grins and grimaces, a few glares, but most of them are blank. The team is a vacant stare, a blank curtain of shielded humanity. My copy hangs over my desk to this day, but does little to inspire me.

When the cheesy photographer scampered away I told the guys to stay put, and fetched my camera from the car. I wanted a different sort of image. The players immediately relaxed, remaining in their rows but bubbling now with more of their natural adolescent fizz. In part, this shows a desire to humor me, their coach; but we always emphasized that they play to please each other, and I think that shows, too. Issuing no orders, I just began snapping away. As I shifted off to their left, they shifted too, the formality of the forced event dissolving as the team settled into more natural postures and expressions. The resulting photograph — the best one of the bunch I made — parts the curtain to reveal more of this group's character. The team cutups are cutting up: Jesse Hall looking like the cat who's swallowed the canary; Dan Campbell belly-laughing at his own rude joke; Mitch McDonald leaning forward and holding his chosen tough-guy pose, his adamant individuality now crowned by the only white hat in the crowd. The back-row soldiers are all grinning — Mike and Frankie Swonger, Jay Fannin, Matt Cochis, Dustin Delgouffre and Andrew Smith — their loads seemingly lightened. Sean Swonger has dropped down into the seat I vacated, giggling while his cousin T.J. Turner wears his usual game-face front and center — the brim of his cap carefully bent to form a roof for his eyes. Adam Barcus holds his catcher's crouch and familiar smile; Andy Horn has his shy-guy soul in full shine, smiling and looking down, his hands clasped in a beatific gesture that befits him. And off at the far left edge, deep in the shadows and low to the ground, Trevor Gill bends over with his right arm bracing his head, gazing straight at the lens, keen and curious, uncertain but willing. In this image they clearly comprise a team — an uneven mix of personalities, comfortable in their skin, ready to take it out onto the field and dance to the beat of a baseball game.

And their dancing has slowly improved. In our first season two years back they were a hapless bunch, discovering diverse ways to lose but showing up week after week for more. Their parents sat on the sidelines, alternately laughing, cajoling, cheering on their little victories, consoling them after each loss. As Little League parents go, they were remarkably good-natured. Other teams took delight in profiting from our constant mistakes, but as losing was our pattern, we fostered pride regardless of outcome, demanding heads-up sportsmanship in shaking the other teams' hands afterwards. Look them in the eye, we said. As their coaches we wanted them to win, but more than that, we wanted them to want to win, because good play follows such desire just as good feelings follow good actions. A team can go nowhere until it gets a taste of winning; once that appetite takes hold and becomes familiar, play rises to locate it and recover it. Each game starts 0–0. Hope springs eternal, with good reason.

Our head coach Ron Fannin is a gentle soul who employs an earnest and positive urgency to coax his players onward. As his assistant, I take a more direct and tougher approach, always positive but more challenging. Together we strike a working balance. Ron and I know without ever having discussed it that a positive approach works best, and with that intent we exploit all opportunities to build on the happy accidents that figure each player's best efforts. Small positives grow into new patterns, and good play can become contagious. The only thing we forbid is blame; play as a team, win as a team is what we always say.

And true to form, it begins to happen — one small victory at a time. Gradually the players stop peering at us in the dugout for approval and begin paying more attention to each other out there on the field. Their comradely eye contact begins to define encouragement and determination as they learn to shake off errors and pick up their teammates' spirits, making the recovery plays so crucial to stopping opponents' rallies and getting a grip on victory.

From the high ledge of so-called adulthood it's easy to get sentimental about kids finding their way into the game and discovering their own abilities. But it's a fallacy to mistake youthful experience for something tinged by a soft, warm glow. Parents may settle into a maudlin revery while watching their kids, but the kids themselves battle fears and flight instincts in those moments, edging ever closer to the courage that keeps them in front of a bounding grounder or sends them winging after a sinking linedrive, putting body and soul on the line. Young play is full of willful, hopeful sacrifice, of knowing how much a hardball can hurt but learning from experience that the hurting stops, that pain can be shaken off and that true effort more often results in success. What can't be shaken off is cowardice, the memory of a grounder passing under your legs because you flinched, because you pulled your head up out of the way. A black eye or broken teeth may result from staying down on the ball; but better that than a broken soul. The world is harsh in the face of such dilemmas. So mothers cringe on the sidelines, and fathers grit their teeth and wince at the memories of their own trials reenacted by their sons; but the sons earn some dignity in risk, taking the leap to overcome fear. The world demands such courage, raising the stakes again and again to test it.

In that first season I watched Trevor Gill surrender to fear and suffer its bitter consequences. Trevor was young for his age, the smallest kid in the group. This thirteen-to-fifteen-year-old span of Babe Ruth League ball is a curious mix of little boys and young men, the barely pubescent up against adolescents with much bigger bodies. The squeaky ones struggle from the baby side of that boundary, not yet capable of the physical demands of the full-sized game; they sometimes become the objects of awkward cruelties from the bigger ones. Trevor had the fair-haired look of a little brother trying to catch up, uncertain of his ability but sure of his desire. Again and again he'd retreat from a ball hit hard in his direction, giving in to his first reflex to flee. We tried him at various positions— second base, right field — but his discomfort was always evident. There was nowhere on the field to hide him. We'd hand him the lightest bat in the bag, but he still struggled to swing it.

What makes such a kid continue? Surely, the dream of getting there. His was a losing battle — he'd always flinch before catching himself and trying to recover. But by then the ball was past him. He was very tough on himself, dropping his head in shame after each blown play, sagging on the bench with disconsolate sorrow. We'd pat him on the back and tell him "don't worry, man — go get the next one." It was as if he was facing a hill within himself, a mound he desperately wanted to cross, but his first hesitant step always undercut his chances of vaulting over it. He was not yet free of the fear, and it cost him dearly.

It cost the team, too. There were times when we just couldn't put Trevor out there, knowing his fear could create an avalanche of errors in the others. Truth is, none of them, not even those whose voices had deepened, were all the way over the hill. Their determination was fragile; fear and failure can spread quickly among young guys.

To his credit, Trevor always wanted to be in the game. He suffered his bench innings badly, and always wore his mitt while he sat there, itching to sprint out to right field on a nod. Even as we held him back, what made us believe he would finally cross that rise was this anger he had — at himself, surely, but also at us. He wanted another chance, demanding to be tested, and while he never pleaded his case verbally, he would sit there and glare at me. It was as if he knew that one good jump would leave the hill behind him, and life from then on would be bathed in new light. He was tired of failing, and could taste the gritty satisfaction that success would bring. When I'd stroll past him on the bench and offer my hand for a low-five slap, he'd slap it hard, then pound his mitt.

To his teammates' credit, they also believed he'd cross the great divide. Straddling it themselves, they wanted him over on their side. His success would bolster their own, convincing them that the fears they witnessed in him could be defeated in themselves.

The Navy Seals, we told them, never leave a wounded man on the beach; as one goes, we all go. Our pre-game ritual of the Indian Run reinforced this belief: a team is only as fast as its slowest man, only as strong as its weakest link. We'd run a lap around the entire park in a line (coaches included); as we jogged along, the last man in line sprinted up to take the lead, and set the pace until the next last man took his place. This is not a race, we told them; you're not here to beat each other out, but to run the lap as a team. It's up to the lead man to make sure the pace allows that. One by one, we were all the last man, sprinting past our teammates to take the lead and set the right pace for all to follow. When the group reached the left-field foul pole, it was an all-out, hell-bent sprint for the dugout, and time to play ball.

And play they did. Adam, Sean, Andrew, T.J., Mike, Frankie, Dustin, Matt, Mitch, Jay, Dan, Jesse and Andy all crossed the hill together; and Trevor reached the top in the last inning of the last game of the season, sprinting for a flyball in right, settling under it, and holding steady as it spun into his glove for what was arguably the greatest catch ever made. His team hoisted him up and carried him off the field. The crowd of parents savored their sentiments, wiping their eyes and patting each other on the back.

Our generous team sponsors are Bobby and Roger, who run the Village Market in Gambier. Both are former Babe Ruth players from way back when. The market is a genial place, locally famous for its 50-cent hot dogs. These Market Dogs provide sustenance for hungry farmers in town on errands and Kenyon students heading to the library for study. The saintly market mother Marianne alternates her time between the front checkout and the deli counter at the back of the store, where she wraps Market Dogs in waxed paper with a sly eye and a knowing smile. It's all wrapped up with the fact of constancy in this little village; students and faculty come and go, farmers live and die with the vagaries of weather, and the world suffers under fire and ice; but even now, in this day and age, if you're nearly broke and famished you can get a Market Dog and live to do what you must.

Thanks to the largesse of the Bobby and Roger we wear the Cleveland colors, but in my mind the Gambier Village Market Indians will always be The Market Dogs— sustained by the generous spirit of their community and their own best instincts. Old hound that I am, I'll feast on that sentiment 'til the day I die, watching them run like a pack of pups, surpassing fear to locate home just over the next big hill.

Original

There is no single point of origin, they now say. The researchers hunkered in the library at Cooperstown arrive at this agreement by way of unsettling the argument: where was baseball invented, and who invented it?

It comes to us from all manner of forebears— Manhattan gentlemen playing afield in the Victorian manner, keeping the rabble out. Then after the Civil War the working men, gritty factory types, guys with the sweat of their workday still on them. Peppery Englishmen and their wickets, decked out in bright whites. Country boys in rags with barrel staves and city kids ruling a side street, three manholes deep.

Hunks of balled-up cotton and leather, rubber, and other industrial sorts.

It comes up from the ground and hangs here. We shape it to our uses, its definition always reflecting larger fields as it focuses us on the demands of particular play on a given day. Most clearly it comes up from youth, organizing itself into a fashion that yearns toward a higher form as it choreographs its own.

The most useful origin of baseball is the one you find in your own time. All of the effort you make to achieve it at any level, and any age, becomes the wellspring of your game, locating all that you need to know. The game invites you in as a true original, with origins. Your own experience counts the most.

Purpose-Pitch

I didn't write this.

The purpose of this program is to prepare the individual pitcher in each of the eight areas that relate to pitching success.

A. MECHANICS
B. STUFF
C. CONDITIONING
D. VELOCITY
E. IDENTITY
F. MATURITY
G. ATTITUDE / MIND-SET
H. WILL TO PREPARE

I keep that mambo-jambo on my office wall as a shrine to the baseball mind (or, "mind-set") as it tends to be expressed by college and high-school coaches everywhere. The set's order seems quite random; it doesn't map to any sequence of actions actually undertaken in pitching and winning. Its abstractions of purpose are like litter, empty paper cups blowing around in a swirling wind. They're meant to help a pitcher understand his task, but they just circle distractedly around it.

Nowhere in there does it say anything about winning. If the goal is to play a winning game (the best kind of game, the only satisfying result, and the most useful goal) then all of these abstractions have to be banished. No mistake, they must also be accomplished; not in this order or with these words, but with rote focus, with the will to do it again and better, the will not just to prepare but to prevail, to win each pitch as game-within-game. Lacking that — not the will so much as the doing — you find loss and loss and loss, even as you check off the whole list of A. through H in your head. The game, alas, is played on a field. The game in your mind is something else entirely.

There are coaches who maintain that winning is everything (the only thing). They're wrong, and they're right. Wrong-headed in implying that all the particular manifestations of the game are nothing, and the final score is all that matters. We know there's more to it than that. For one thing, dealing with loss in a graceful way to help yourself (and those around you) put it away and go for the next win is something any coach needs to resolve, because it matters.

But they're right in the sense that knowing how to win — like you know gravity — is the right way to play, and the way to be remembered, whether in the mind of big history like the 1998 Yankees or in the memory of a neighborhood. With winning understood thoughtlessly, with a minute-by-minute, pitch-by-pitch enactment of that urgency made plain in well-focused play, the game becomes a beholden beauty and a beauty to behold. And the beauty endures.

◆

The purpose-pitch is the best illustration of how pitching is done and undone. Like other baseball chestnuts, it's a troublesome term: each pitch should have purpose, not just the purpose-pitch. But the notion that a pitcher should know when and how to throw at a batter to regain physical and psychological control of the strike zone is a sound one, and the purpose-pitch surely has its place — hard-in on the body of a would-be slugger. When delivered with good timing and design, it communicates belief. The pitcher owns the plate for the whole inning; each batter is just an interloper, a visitor entitled to no hospitality. If he looks too comfortable up there, too at-home as it were, crowding the plate and taking big hacks, it's best to remind him who's throwing the ball where, and how hard. An effective pitcher sends constant, hard-cut messages of "I'm here to spoil your day." The losing trap a pitcher can fall into is all about missing with pitches, falling behind in counts and giving a batter opportunities to realize his own purpose. And there's nothing more shattering for a pitcher than leaving his purpose-pitch where that hitter can knock it out of the park. Such reversal of fortune can snap a pitcher's neck.

All purposeful pitches send messages of command. Throwing a pitch without purpose, without preparation, without good mechanics, stuff, conditioning, velocity, identity, maturity, attitude, mind-set, and will, is just like spitting on yourself. Good pitching takes the hard road to win, with no shortcuts. It's muscled up in memory with thought rooted in synapse, wanting to continue, to succeed. Spiritus sancti, forever and ever amen, good pitching is blessed, body and soul in each moment with the shine of a pending win on your skin and the ball in your hand.

So, if I were making an A. through H. list for pitchers, here's what I'd put on it:

A. WIN THIS
Stay in the present, and take each small victory one by one.

B. ROTE CONDITIONING
Rote comes from the Middle English: a traveled way. By rote, by memory alone, without thought. Working with practiced mental quiet makes it easier to do the same in a game. A chattering mind only slows down the circuits.

C. BE THERE
Everything flows from a pitcher's presence on the mound.

D. WIND-UPS, MECHANICS & GRIPS
Practiced by rote, beyond thought, with purpose — always striving for good results the same way.

E. SPEED & STUFF
Get the best from good mechanics— throw hard, locate, make pitches move.

F. STRIKE ZONES
Every umpire has one. Learn it and earn it.

G. TEAM
Lead by example.

H. EACH WIN IS A STEP UP
Each pitch, each play, each inning is a rising battle to win.

Then I'd crumple it up and toss it away. Let's go throw.

Said

"Losing is the spooky music that runs under baseball," wrote Thomas Boswell, sports columnist for *The Washington Post*, who has his ear to the ground.

"Good luck is what is left over after intelligence and effort have combined at their best ... Luck is the residue of design." That was Branch Rickey speaking of his 1952 Pittsburgh Pirates, of whom he also said: "They finished last — on merit."

Yogi said it best: "We were overwhelming underdogs." He was talking about the Amazin' Mets of 1969, who got rich slowly, giving to get. You don't have to reach the bigs to have a brilliant career. You just have to give it all.

Turtle Disease

Otherwise known as the yips, or getting Sax'd, Turtle Disease is the nightmare of any player who's ever had it. It's a neurological tic that becomes hard-wired, causing your baby throws to red-shift away in horror, your arm's range and control suddenly gone bye-bye. It's magnetic, or so it can seem: earth's liquid core takes a slide and so your easy throw to first sails high and wide, or a simple toss to second flutters into left field like a drunken seagull. With an existential gasp you lose control over basic motor mechanics — you lock up, all nerve gone awry. And it perpetuates to your next throw. You begin to hesitate as you cock your arm, trying too hard to get it right this time, and the result is straight down into the dirt, or high over someone's head. It's ugly, and devastating, and very hard to shake.

Major leaguers are not immune. Steve Sax is the prototype — a solid defensive player whose throws from second base suddenly devolved into these gasping meltdowns. Steve Blass, a frontline starting pitcher for years, went from force to farce in the blink of an eye — had it one season, the next spring couldn't buy a strike, ever again. Mackey Sasser caught for the Mets and had a fine arm — could nail baserunners with strong, accurate throws. But he couldn't get the ball back to the pitcher after each pitch — that was where the yips got him.

He'd tap the ball in his mitt, fake a throw or two, change grips, then lob it short, bringing an annoyed pitcher down off the mound again. Runners finally started pulling delayed steals on him, taking off as he gagged over the ball. A legitimate slash hitter, he was gone from the bigs in no time.

The worst case I ever witnessed up-close was at an ancient ruins of a ballpark — Gerig Park, the old New York Giants spring training camp on the decidedly dark Westside of Ocala, Florida. This crumbling fortress, surrounded by 12-foot stone walls, featured a standard sacred baseball diamond and a small grandstand behind home. But the outfields were huge. The left-field wall was over 400 feet from home plate; dead center was so deep they had a practice infield out there. The sense of history was also immense — Mel Ott's ghost rolling his eyes in the dugout.

We were there to try out for the Indianapolis Clowns, a barnstorming team revived from its 1950s heydey — Hank Aaron's first pro team. The Clowns did a baseball roadshow in the deep tradition of Negro League barnstormers; only now, with a mix of black, Hispanic and white players, the shadowball was mostly a product of the coaching staff working clown acts between innings. The wheelchair-bound manager gave hitting clinics and demonstrations after the games. The Clowns traveled by bus all summer, living a hard carny sort of life, and settled here in Ocala in winter to train, try out new players, and run clinics.

The Clowns could really play, so the tryout was a momentous challenge for us. We brought seven Stony Brook Cardinals, including Uncle Rosie; Goldy; George, of course, in the three-hole; myself; and our catcher Turtle, a small sparkplug of a player who had been a steady contributor in our Cardinal campaigns. Rob Marto came as well, along with Mark Napoli, another pitcher from the Suffolk Stan Musial league.

We had just completed some running and stretching when the head Clown told us to throw on the sidelines, to get loose for infield/outfield drills. We paired off— me and Rosie, Goldy with George, and Turtle with one of the pitchers. We stood in lines thirty feet from each other and began soft tossing. From the get-go, Turtle just couldn't get a grip — one throw was short, the next one high and wide. With the Clowns looking on, the yips took him over. No one said anything at first, but after a few minutes of this, as we began to spread out for longer throws, his got worse and worse — his partner having to lunge in for a low hop, then sprint back to retrieve a long overthrow.

Turtle finally shook his head and walked away with the ball. His plan was to get himself right by throwing against one of the high walls. His first toss sailed right out of the Gerig Park and he turned to dust, right there.

To his credit, Turtle battled back. While that tryout was a goner, he eventually prevailed over his disease and played successfully for many more seasons. Marto and Napoli were signed that week and became true Clowns, touring that summer all across the states, playing against local all-star teams and semipros. The rest of us ground out another Cardinal season back on Long Island, aware that the Turtle Disease could fester forth at any time in any of us, unforseen and unforgiving. It makes you want to pull your head inside your shell and never come out. And the only known cure is a mix of two parts blind determination and one part amnesia — with your head out, seeing it finally right.

Would-Be Wolf

Like other state capitols Columbus, Ohio, has a strange underlying calm about it; these government centers tend to lack the commercial buzz and cultural drive of, say, a Cleveland. But for years (for some odd reason) greater Columbus has served as a testbed for all manner of "new" "consumer" "products." It is here that Americans first bought premade icecream cones in convenience stores, for example; the icecream, nuts and chocolate syrup already attached to the cone, frozen, wrapped in an ingenious paper triangle that peels away from the icecream but not the cone, thus providing a serviceable, sanitary holder in the American mode. Other handy items have also debuted here, in the postwar crackle and crunch of our so-called economy. Perhaps it's that Columbus people are statistically-ideal consumers by some set of metrics; there are, it seems, more obese people here than anywhere I've ever been — eager to unwrap the new, they may be somewhat more than statistically-ideal. For all these reasons, Columbus is sometimes referred to by its more ironic residents as Velveetaville. It has the cheesy quality of a handily-wrapped, bright-shiny box, neatly stacked and easy to open, loaded with certain nutrients and lacking others.

Living not far from Columbus in my bucolic village, I'm sauced by the call of Velveetaville baseball. Clearly, my skills would not pass muster in Minnesota townball (at least not the A-division); maybe not in the Twilight League either. But I do have this hope of playing again this year, after taking last summer off. The decision to hang them up is thus put off again, still. I need to work my legs into game-shape, but I've got some energy left; I've been throwing against the fieldhouse wall all winter, and my stuff is (sometimes) sharp. And (sometimes) not. Like cheese.

I don't want to go back to the MSBL Angels/Warthogs— that scene sort of played itself out. And I've been wondering how I'd fare against middling younger talent in the MABL — the 21-and-over guys. For sure, there'd be some good players there — some college guys, lots of mid-twenties working men, young dads and goofy post-teens. But there'd also be just-plain ballplayers. Guile only gets you so far in this game, but I feel like I've got enough (vain hope) left to have one more fine season somewhere. At least some moments to sparkle. Then maybe I'll pack it in.

So these are my thoughts (for now, unspoken) as I compete for a spot on the Columbus Wolves roster for this 2000 season. It's another new team, and I'm coming in fresh and unproven, wanting to find a way to contribute.

I found the Wolves on the Internet, in true Y2K fashion. They compete in the Central Ohio Baseball League under the MABL umbrella and rules. They were the only team with their own Web page, and I liked the name: Columbus Wolves— a fine counterpoint to the whole Velveetaville thing. They finished last season in the middle of their division, so they're neither a powerhouse nor a bunch of lower-case clowns.

The Wolves play their games in Reynoldsburg, just east of Columbus and close to where I work. I used their Web page to send an e-mail expressing interest in trying out with them. A small blizzard of messages ensued between me and Jason, one of their coaching triumvirate. I told him about playing at Kenyon from '94 through '96 and he naturally assumed I was younger, but with each message it began to dawn on him that something didn't add up. His dogged e-mail questions finally ran me to ground. From the first note all I'd asked for was a tryout — no commitments 'til you see me (and I see you, I didn't say). But when I revealed that I was 47 he began begging off — we really need younger guys— trying to get over the top, etc. So I called him on it — literally called him on the phone finally, getting his dad's number as Jason's was unlisted. We talked. I wore him down, finally getting his reluctant agreement that I could show up for a Wolf workout at an indoor batting cage in Westerville, Ohio, where they'd give me a look.

The following Sunday I showed up for the workout with great expectations, determined to overcome the whole age thing. I walked into Grand Slam Baseball in sweats with my head up, ready to sweat, and did some stretching off on the side while the Wolves gathered. I shook their hands, introduced myself all around, and was invited by the triumvirate (Jason, Charles and Bumper) to throw some batting practice. I wanted to throw off a mound for them, and show them some stuff while I still had some, but instead got to the task of hurling BP for the boys. It's not a bad way to size up a pitcher, actually — having him throw to real batters, without a catcher. It's hard to do well unless you're not just flexible, but downright adjustable.

BP is key for other reasons, and has always been a sore point with me: local teams tend to do a lot of it, but not very well. They lob the ball in to their hitters and watch them wail, drilling the sorts of far-too-easy pitches they'll never see in a game. My approach has always been to throw hard in BP — not pitching to try to get guys out, but giving them straight hittable fastballs right in the zone with some gitty-up on them. It's much more valuable practice that way; and it's best yet when hitters don't stay in the cage for 20 swings at a time, but get a few hacks and get out of the way for the next guy to jump in. Crisp BP develops good hitting in a team, I have no doubt. Soft and sloppy practice goes nowhere. The Cardinals used to drive me nuts with that — George would get 15 guys out for a practice and spend 3 hours doing nothing but soft-slow-sloppy BP — a real snoozer. I used to lobby him to do infield practice first, to get ourselves some defensive work before we settled in for eternal swings. He wanted none of it, being there himself purely to hit and hit some more. And typically, once BP began, the end was clear — guys would drift off eventually with George up there for the fifth time, pulling scarred baseballs over the left-field fence, a glazed outfielder merely looking up to watch them fly overhead. Paralytic.

The other thing about BP is that I could never throw consistent strikes by lobbing the ball. I need to throw hard to get rhythm and locate.

So I threw to the Wolves, a couple sets, probably 100 BP pitches, and would've done more but they stopped me. I gave the hitters some great swings, yelling at them to lay off the balls and hit strikes. They liked it. I got a few swings myself, and didn't show much, but my timing was just off and I wasn't really feeling the bat-head yet — hadn't swung all winter. I think they saw that I'd come around. I insisted on throwing about 15 more pitches off the mound to their catcher, Bob, then they shut me down. I had the clear sense that I'd made the team before I ever threw those pitches to Bob. The Wolves seemed to have some understanding of how the game is played, perhaps won. I believed I could contribute, and they believed my belief.

♦

We've worked out a half-dozen times since then, once outdoors on a blessed 70-degree Sunday afternoon in early March. Now we're back in the cage, with the Ohio weather having returned to more usual springtime form. It's a bastard when you've been outside and you have to come back in for workouts. The batting cages are tough places to assemble 15 guys into some form of reasonable practice. The way the Wolves do it is, we get in the cage and throw in pairs as we show up; guys straggle in and take their turns, two by two. Not everyone thus warms up, but the pitchers do, and the others do some stretching and dry swings in the hallway. Then we throw BP from behind an L-screen, feeding batting-practice strikes to our hitters, and they blister them. This team can really hit, at least in the cage, and I suspect they will in games. Once we get a round or two of 15 swings each, we start this game where each batter has to lay down a bunt, then hit-and-run the next pitch (wherever), then go to work. To continue hitting you have to hit the ball fair; grounders are OK but popups are out. You can hit flyballs high and deep to keep going, but if you hit the top net anywhere in front of the pitcher, you're out. One batted-ball out or swing-and-miss and you're gone. We count how many hits in a row each guy gets, and usually the winner has a 20-hit tear, sometimes more, before the BP pitcher bears down and starts trying to get him out.

We rotated, five of us, in throwing to the hitters. Cage pitchers have only agility and the L-screen to protect them from flying hardballs. When aluminum alloy bats meet BP stuff, baseballs rocket. The soft netting of the sides and top of the cage eat the ball's energy, but when a ball hits a cage post it can carom off and get you. BP pitchers learn to use the L-screen for cover, finishing their deliveries by ducking down behind its tall side. Since the cage is so narrow (barely 15 feet across, 15 feet high, and 70 feet deep) hitters try to blast the ball up the middle. That's the only way you can really read how you've hit the ball in the cage, when you can see it all the way up the middle, or line it into a back corner. It's the only satisfaction the cage gives you as a hitter.

The L-screen is thus a satisfying target, because it means you're drilling something at the pitcher — which, in a game, is a good way to make him sweat. We had a stud hurler show up one week — someone's friend-of-a-friend — and throw BP all-out, off the mound. This goon threw hard, and it really wasn't BP at all — it was him showing off as a pitcher. The triumvirate put up with it because the guy was sort of an alpha wolf — big and muscle-bound and aggressive. He was striking guys out left and right — no one getting anything off him. He'd set you up with fastballs then bounce a diving knuckle-curve off the astroturf. After the first round we put on helmets.

The second time through the lineup, hitters starting timing him and getting better swings. I took a fastball up and in then lined the next pitch off the L-screen, right at his eyeballs, and thus earned some respect. Others did likewise. Hercules hasn't been back since, but guys seem to want him on the mound come game-time. I dunno.

♦

For the first few workouts I threw BP from behind the L-screen, short — about 50 feet from home. I threw pretty well, and have since chucked some solid BP — quick hittable strikes right in the zone, though they've been drifting higher as I tire. So I've shown the Wolves I can be hit; it'll take game to show them I can get guys out.

Truth is, the cage is getting old. We need to be outside, no matter the weather, doing something more than what the tunnel allows. This morning, throwing BP, Andy Crabtree took a linedrive off the forehead — Big Charles' liner following young Andy like a tracer as he ducked for the screen, and hitting him near the right temple — quick as a shot. He went down in a heap and we ran in to him, cradling his head and holding his chest to keep him from getting up. He didn't lose consciousness but he was bashed — his forehead swelling in a big nasty welt. We got him some ice, then called the squad and had him checked out before letting him up. The coaches took him to the hospital just to be safe, on the advice of the squad, and called his parents. It was scary.

By the time they left for the ER we had only 20 minutes left, so I jumped behind the screen and threw some more BP. But most of the collective heart was gone from it. I threw hard, deliberately not giving guys fat pitches to hit, and I danced behind that screen like a scared monkey when they smacked comebackers. In 15 minutes we were done and I had a good sweat going.

With any luck we'll be outside next week. I'll lobby for that, weather notwithstanding. We need to run around and find the game's real measure. As they like to say here in Velveetaville, where in their peculiar Ohio idiolect infinitives are bane: these wolves need uncaged.

♦

I got my wish the following Sunday. The weather was touch-and-go all week — our skies gray-clad, rainy, too cool — but on Saturday the clouds broke and the temps soared to the mid–50s, and Sunday ever-much-moreso. I got to Spangler Field early and had it all to myself. There was a stiff late-winter wind sweeping from left field to right, shifting now and again to blow straight out to center. The field grass was greening in the slanted sunlight. Spangler's turf is nothing to write home to mama about — not a polished gem but a rough one, clumpy, its bare spots spangled by tough fists of grass. But in this light, upon this day, it sure looked good. We'd soon see how it plays.

Bumper arrived with Jason and Charles, saying with a squint "this field needs raked." So we raked. As with everything baseball, Bumper had a sensible system for getting it done, and in no time we had the infield dirt smoothed out and were ready to go.

The game was only a scrimmage, but we had college umps and both teams were eager to rev it up. Our opponents, the Bisons, looked solid in pregame infield/outfield practice, and they came out hitting, scoring several in the second inning. But in the end the day was ours. We beat the mighty Bisons (who went 24–5 last year) by a score of 12–11. I started the game at second, played two innings there and turned a nice tailor-made doubleplay in the first to bring it in scoreless. I had two hits, neither off a sure swing — one a topped dribbler that stopped somewhere way short of third, a classic unintentional swinging bunt that got me to first. I moved to second on a walk, then Jason knocked me in with a rope double into the gap. My other hit was a wind-blown popup single into short center that should have been caught by someone, but nobody quite got there. I scored that inning, too. Not yet having my game-legs, I managed to hippity-skippity home, looking (I felt) like a bit of a fairy. In my other at-bats I popped out and flew out and grounded, a repertoire of batting failure lacking only a strikeout to make it complete. With Irish luck I came away 2-for-5, a solid .400 in the book despite all awkwardness. One can only work for such luck, the residue.

Bumper started the game on the mound and went 4 innings. He was hit but he also pitched well, settling down, throwing some quality strikes, getting out of jams and keeping us in the game. He finished the 4th with a gutsy strikeout of a dangerous hitter, then dropped onto the dugout bench and gave me the nod. I threw the next two innings, with more good fortune: 1 hit, 1 unearned run, 3 strikeouts, 3 walks. The walks I'm not proud of, but then, I was giving hitters nothing to hit and keeping them off-balance. When you do that, unless the ump loves you, you're gonna walk some guys. Those 3 walks just showed more disciplined hitting, those batters waiting for a pitch they could hit and never getting one. The strikeout victims didn't get one either. The curveball was working, the changeup was diving, and my so-called fastball had a little wiggle. I stayed out of the heart of the zone but close enough to its frame to get some corners and make them swing at tough spots. It was hot-diggety-shit, and I loved it.

On your first outing of the season you feel a bit like an alien on the mound — it's a round and very exposed little planet in low-earth orbit. I felt the dizziness of the unfamiliar out there — that slight psychic imbalance—but the indoor work paid off with mechanical steadiness, some rhythm, and a sense of sure distance from the floating target. I felt weightless, but able to breathe. Deep breathing is key, and it's what I'll do better next time.

♦

Next time, however, is rain. Our next Sunday dawns soaking wet, the lost-hour morning at the start of Daylight Savings Time (which ought to be a national holiday, by the way) gone to mud. I'm up early, sitting at the window with a mug of coffee, lamenting all such tragedy. Rainouts are another sort of kick-in-the-gut heartbreaker. They run down your back with the cold trickle of no-play-today, a sinking sense of abandonment. For me, a rainout always recalls our six-hour drive to Cooperstown with the Shoreham Mets, when we were imprisoned by a two-day drizzle as we pined for the ghosts on Doubleday Field. We were bitter, but when we finally ran onto the field Sunday afternoon, life suddenly sweetened.

Now the rain falls as all such rain through all of time. This too shall pass. For today, it looks like the fieldhouse wall and some wind sprints on a rubber floor—the game's consolation prizes—are all I get.

♦

My next outing—in another scrimmage, this time against the Rockies—I was hit harder, giving up three singles and two earned runs over two innings. I felt distracted out on the mound, forgetting to do basic things like grip the ball properly. It's amazing how you can do that—lose your sense of where you are and what, precisely, you're doing. Bumper and Jason bellowed at me from the bench and I finally got my concentration down, pitching out of a jam in my second inning, then shutting it down. I'll do better next time out. I was less effective with two weeks between outings; I need to throw more mid-week to be on the ball come Sunday.

We blew a big lead but won that scrim in the end. We're undefeated now, and none of it counts.

The Wolves, I must admit, are unexpected—more than what I hoped for, so far. A good enough/bad enough team to have room for me at 47, despite all sight-unseen reservations. Guys who have enough of the game to know its limits and see daylight when it shows up. I'm not going to put them over the top, but I can contribute, and want to, and they can see the value in that.

◆

I debated with myself over getting a new glove — another good one. I've had several, including my original Rawlings Heart of the Hide, but one of my Yanqui brothers borrowed it and it came back torn. I've played with it since, but worry sometimes about that big tear across the top of the pocket, how a ball might find that. My real gamer was gone. I'm ashamed to admit it, but I lost my game glove — a fine little Mizuno middle-infielder's model — leaving it on the dugout roof when I walked away from what proved to be my last game with the Angels.

What I needed was a new glove. People might say a new mitt; but the only mitts allowed in baseball are those used by catchers and first basemen. They're mitts in the sense that all the fingers are together in one section, like a mitten. Other position players use baseball gloves, with separate fingers like any glove.

I looked at lesser models in a department store and bought one for Adam, our Market Dog catcher and pitcher who'd just made his high school junior varsity team. It was better by a good bit than what he had, and I didn't figure he was quite ready to need a $150 gamer. I didn't buy one for myself, because I already had several just as good, not good enough.

The sheer longing for a good new gamer hit me one night when I was asleep, and when I awoke the decision had been made to go get one. I found Kelley Baseball and their product line on the Web and ordered an LR1000 middle infielder's glove — a small black one with a complex web and just enough pocket.

◆

As you walk on to each new level of play, at any age, you have to get better. Even if your play dazzles everyone for a game or two, or for part of a season, the work must not only continue but step up a notch. You can't hibernate and not get better. It happens with major-league Joe Blow rookies — they get to the bigs mid-season, play well, and think they've made it. They go home and relax, do a lot of celebrating. When they show up the next spring there are other guys knocking on that same door, and if Joe hasn't made himself better, hasn't raised his game noticeably, he's likely to lose his shot and be shipped back to the bush.

The same thing happens in the amateurs, though without the professional consequences. Moving up a competitive level is nothing more than a reason to get better than you are, better than you've ever been. There is the real possibility of being better older than you were younger — I've seen it happen. The world is full of late bloomers, and while age surely slows you down, when you net it out, it does not necessarily degrade you. You can be better, eclipsing what you were when you didn't know.

The accumulation of knowing makes aging wonderful. Ask any random sampling of players, pro or bush, and they're likely to tell you they'd only go back in years if they could go knowing what they know now. Youth isn't worth the loss of all the games and years, and knowing how much more there is to know.

♦

Another rained-out scrimmage and we're good to go. Our season opens next week against the Vipers, who beat the Wolves in last year's opener. It's time to rain some just revenge upon those snakes. Now it all counts.

League of Dreams

It's local baseball. A very pure form, in fact. Pay-to-play; age brackets; wood-bat weekends. Games on bright Sundays and under the lights on weeknights. The Men's Senior Baseball League is a thriving enterprise with 40,000 players under its umbrella in affiliated leagues coast-to-coast. And it came to be by virtue of one bright guy who had an idea and took it beyond his dreams.

When I joined the Stony Brook Cardinals in 1985 they were more organized than the other pick-up teams they were playing on a regular basis. But there was one player among those others who had a vision — a dream actually — of making this small random sampling of over-30 Sunday ballplayers into a real league. What Steve Sigler saw was this: that age is the great leveler, and that lots of guys still young in their thirties would love to play ball against others equally young and variously able. That they could, in fact, have the time of their lives in resuming the real game, competing and finding comradery among their like and opposite numbers.

The voice in Steve's head whispered something like this: build it and they will come. He set about to build not a field but a league of dreams, with much the same miraculous spirit as that enacted in Ray Kinsella's cornfield. Drawing players from local softball leagues then from a wider population of weekend athletes, the MSBL has since created a home for thousands of guys who still want to play the game, but who might not want to compete against 18-year-olds. Against their own kind, there is glory. Field of Dream's final scene, with the endless line of headlights approaching Ray's self-made heaven, is just what the league of dreams truly did.

Steve began the process by putting a small banner ad in the classified section of Newsday, seeking would-be baseball players over the age of 30. It was not a unique idea — Ken Robinson and George had formed the Stony Brook Cardinals that way a few years earlier — but Steve had the over–30 vision. As he assembled those first few league meetings, Steve and the gathered flock found ways to recast certain rules to enable older guys a better experience of the game: players would be allowed to sit an inning or two and re-enter. This free defensive substitution meant that more guys would get innings and managers could freely juggle their position players to keep everyone happy. The batting order was sacrosanct — the lineup could not be juggled during a game — but it could be as long as you wanted, so if you chose, you could bat everybody. Teams thus could spread the wealth and share the load of playing the game, using more players to avoid injuries, hurt feelings and exhaustion. Pitchers and catchers could opt for pinch-runners, and in fact, most any limping player could get a runner if he needed one. Otherwise, the game's rules stood as they do elsewhere. To the delight of those first players, it was the real game and they were inside it again.

The four original MSBL teams included Sigler's Jericho Mets and George's Stony Brook Cardinals. Toward the end of that 1986 season Newsday ran a story in its sports section about the league, and Steve made sure the story carried his phone number. He got 250 calls in the next few days, and the ball was rolling.

Word spread fast. Steve continued advertising, and began finding entire teams wanting to come in. He organized open-tryout drafts for single players to find teams and for teams to fill out their rosters. The league went from four teams in 1986 to 17 teams the next year, to 40 the next. Like a rocket. The devoted followers helped in finding fields, getting deals on equipment, and spreading the gospel. Steve and his wife Connie organized a challenge tournament against Tom Hayden's Los Angeles team, and the expanding MSBL universe was quickened by a July 4th, 1988 article in Sports Illustrated. In the following two weeks they got 2,500 calls. The MSBL provided guidance and structure to leagues forming all over the country, using Steve's method — advertise locally, get a small league going, and watch it grow.

For the autumn of 1987 the idea was to go national with an open tournament in Phoenix. All over–30 teams and leagues from across the country were welcome. Securing the use of major-league spring training facilities all around the greater Phoenix and Tucson areas, that first MSBL World Series sparked the over–30 zeitgeist — 38 teams and 500 players spending a week in the sun doing nothing but baseball. They went away dazzled and told their friends. Today, the MSBL Phoenix World Series and the Fall Classic in Florida are the largest amateur baseball tournaments in the world. In 1999 the MSBL ran the baseball division of the Nike World Games in Oregon, putting its organizing muscle to work on behalf of fine competition for the very best international amateurs. They've managed to make all manner of baseball available for multitudes— working men and their families, former pros not fading away, and earnest players still feeling their oats long after they thought the harvest was in.

The league of dreams now comprises almost 3,000 teams in 300 local organizations across the U.S. and in the Far East, Australia, Central America and Europe. When the powerhouse Kang-Tu team from Taiwan lost the Little League World Series to the upstart Trumbull, Connecticut, in August 1989, Steve got a call the very next day from an over–30 Taiwanese team, seeking an invitation to go for the MSBL gold in Phoenix that November. The Taiwans came at their own expense, delighted their tournament opponents with sharp and sincere play, and left without the gold but with great dignity and many gift souvenirs. They traded jerseys with their hosts and went home with authentic ones from all over local America.

The MSBL was a stroke of genius, preceded perhaps in various places by other local leagues, but in Steve Sigler's hands organized and promoted on a remarkable scope. It now includes an 18-and-over division (the MABL, in which the Wolves compete among 16,000 players nationwide); there are over–30, over–40 and over–50 divisions playing locally and in the national tournaments. Numerous ex–pro players compete, and the competitive levels have sharpened to the point where tournament championships really mean something. Don't go soft, play hardball has always been the slogan, and it was a winning notion. Like the expanding universe, it continues to red-shift outward from Steve's kitchen in Jericho, Long Island, to create the game's occasion, sweeping the national mind like wind in the corn, inviting us all back in.

Closer

Two years after I first met him, Market Dog Andy Horn has grown six inches and sprouted sideburns. His teammates are now calling him Elvis. Whatever else has changed, Andy's manner is still quiet, respectful and earnest; with his brothers he is home-schooled, his mother Angie and his father Rick preparing a nourishing bounty of lessons and home-cooked meals, day by day. Andy's now our starting catcher, and though his throws still arc too high, they now reach second base on the fly. He's gotten very good at blocking pitches in the dirt, learning to trust his shin guards and chest protector and face mask to keep the hard baseball from eating him alive. "Be a wall, Andy!" we yell to him with a runner on third. But in truth we're very glad he is not a wall. We like him as Andy Horn.

The baseball gene has found firmest expression in Andy's little brother Ben. Two years younger than Andy, Ben looks like he's nine, not thirteen. His manner is as shy as his brother's, his build is slight and his voice still squeaks. But boy, can Ben play ball. We've had him at second base, in center field and on the mound, and he does it all.

He looks like he can barely reach the plate when he pitches, but he consistently gets much bigger guys out. He looks like the bat should be swinging him, but he gets the big hits when we need them. What stands out most in Ben is his love of playing this game. Every effort is all-out. From the third base coaching box I've watched him take eager leads off second base, and after each pitch slide back into the bag — never mind that the pitcher, shortstop and second baseman are barely aware he's there. He's there. The game seems to light him up, keeping him in perpetual motion like a wind across grassland. He's one of those kids for whom the game was surely invented. So it was with much satisfied amusement that I heard his young teammates bestow upon him a most befitting nickname — Little Big Horn. It fits him from all angles.

In those same two years Trevor Gill has become a solid second baseman and a two-hole hitter extraordinaire. He's our best bunter and opposite-field hitter, and he hasn't made an error at second all year. His progress is all his own — payday for all the hard work and desire — and he gladly shares it with the rest of us. In our third season, the Market Dogs are 16–2 in the Knox County Baseball League, one of three powerhouse teams headed for the playoffs. We're nobody's joke anymore. It's amazing what can happen when you focus on building skill and forget about winning for awhile. Ron Fannin and I decided to keep things simple and upbeat, and to let the players decide when they wanted to win. This year they have made it plain that they understand how winning is done — despite some very tough ballgames and some moments when it all could easily have fallen apart, we haven't seen a moment of panic in them yet. And for that we are most proud. Of the several players who have set the tone for the entire team, Trevor emerges clearly, along with Adam Barcus, Eddie Fletcher, Andy Horn and Little Big.

♦

As for the older lads, the Wolves, our season has gone just about as well, due largely to Bumper's grit and sense and stuff on the mound. He's a lefty force — our defense has not betrayed him too often, and we've hit enough to win. I've settled into the role of a backup player, getting some innings at second base and on the mound, but more often coaching at first or third. I just can't grind it out like I could even three years ago—the blessed Murphy youth gene finally facing facts and adding just that nudge of slowness to everything I do. Now I ice my knees after each game, along with the shoulder. I can still compete against 25-year-olds, but I have to pick my spots. I'm lucky to play with these guys, and for the most part, the feelings seem reciprocal.

Comes a time. My last outing on the mound is a disaster — brought on in relief, I have none to offer. Tasked with getting but a single out, I give up two hard base hits and then drill a batter in the ass (on an 0-and-2 count, no less). The hook is mercifully quick, and it's time to face reality: my fastball isn't, my curveball doesn't, the cutter's dull and the changeup's meat.

And so the game makes the decision my heart cannot. I'm enjoying long moments of reflection from the bench, and wondering whether I'll ever again be able to really play the game at whatever level — a respectable level — like I once knew I could. It's one true thing I could do, no matter what else was happening. On the afternoon of the day my father died, I shagged flies in the Cardinal outfield and played a blurry game with all I had. Out of respect.

For all the above, I'm grateful. There's more to life than baseball, after all; but without it, my life would have been much less. You don't have to make it to the bigs to have a brilliant career (in your own mind, body and soul). You just have to give it all. And whatever satisfaction lies in that is all you get.

It's enough.

AFTERWORD

My thanks to all those who contributed to Bushville, both in living its stories and guiding its writing. Special thanks go to Peter Rutkoff, Loranne Temple, Phil Brooks, Dan Laskin, Wendy Carlsen and Oscar Will of the Red Door Cafe klatch. Their careful, critical reading helped me find structure. The Kenyon students at the Horn Gallery — most notably Ryan Light and Marela Trejo-Zacarias ("art and justice for all") — graciously granted me opportunities to read portions of the manuscript in performance, for which I'm very grateful. And Bob Creeley, our eminent and gracious American poet, inspires me now as he did when I was his young student. Ron Rosenberg contributed a useful lesson in addition by subtraction. Mike Newell proved that even a football guy can catch the baseball bug. Angelo Pepitone, who has now pitched in five decades, lent his ample memories and some endearing Noo Yawk tawk. Gary Dube, Mitch Swaggert, Kevin Hoy, Bob Philbrick, Fred Schwartz, George Altemose, Jimmy Fogarty, Bob Margolin, Chuck O'Donnell, Rob Santiago and Vince Murray all threw in their share. And the Market Dogs brought it all home.

I never met my grandfather, Joe Murphy, but he provided reason to believe.

SOURCES

Yogi Berra, *The Yogi Book.* New York: Workman Publishing, 1998.
Joseph Campbell, *Mythic Worlds, Modern Words.* New York: HarperCollins, 1993.
Fielding Dawson, *The Greatest Story Ever Told: A Transformation.* Los Angeles: Black Sparrow Press, 1973.
George Gmelch and J.J. Weiner, *In the Ballpark.* Washington D.C.: Smithsonian Institution Press, 1998.
Keith Hernandez and Mike Bryan, *Pure Baseball.* New York: HarperCollins, 1994.
James Joyce, *Finnegans Wake.* New York: Viking Press, 1939.
Rawlings Sporting Goods Company, *Evolutions: Spring 2000 Equipment Catalog.* St. Louis: Rawlings, 1999.
Jim Reisler, *Babe Ruth Slept Here: The Baseball Landmarks of New York City.* South Bend, Indiana: Diamond Communications, 1999.
Jeffrey Scheuer, *The Sound Bite Society.* New York: Four Walls Eight Windows, 1999.
Tom Seaver and Lee Lowenfish, *The Art of Pitching.* New York: Hearst Books, 1984.
Harold Seymour, *Baseball: The People's Game.* New York: Oxford University Press, 1990.
Doug Stewart, "The Old Ball Game," *Smithsonian.* Washington D.C.: Smithsonian Institution, Volume 29 Number 7, October 1998.
John Thorn, *Baseball: Our Game.* New York: Penguin Books, 1995.

INDEX